THE ULTIMATE

BODYBUILDING GUIDE

FOR BEGINNERS

RAIYAMOND RURCHARDE

INTRODUCTION

Welcome to "The Ultimate Bodybuilding Guide for Beginners" – your comprehensive roadmap to transform your body, enhance your fitness journey, and unleash the potential within. This book is more than just a collection of exercises; it's a holistic approach to bodybuilding that combines science, technique, nutrition, and a 12-week jump-start program designed to kickstart your transformation.

Chapter 1: Setting the Foundation

Bodybuilding: Beyond the Aesthetics

Before you embark on this transformative journey, it's crucial to understand that bodybuilding is more than just building muscles for aesthetics. It's about sculpting a healthier, stronger version of yourself. In this chapter, we delve into the philosophy of bodybuilding and how it transcends the physical to impact your mental and emotional well-being.

Understanding Bodybuilding Science

Dive into the science behind bodybuilding – the anatomy, physiology, and biomechanics that form the foundation of effective workouts. By understanding how your body responds to exercise, you'll be equipped to optimize your training and achieve better results.

Setting Personal Goals

Success in bodybuilding begins with setting clear, realistic goals. Learn how to establish goals that align with your aspirations, considering factors such as your current fitness level, lifestyle, and long-term vision. This chapter serves as the compass that guides your entire journey.

Tracking Your Progress

Discover the importance of tracking your progress and how it serves as a powerful motivator. Whether it's measuring muscle growth, strength gains, or improvements in endurance, effective tracking allows you to celebrate victories and adapt your approach when faced with challenges.

Finding Your Gym

Choosing the right gym is a pivotal decision in your bodybuilding journey. Uncover the factors to consider when selecting a gym that suits your needs and provides the right environment for growth.

Learning Essential Techniques

Mastering the fundamental techniques is the key to unlocking the full potential of your workouts. From proper form to breathing techniques, this chapter guides you through the essential skills that will maximize the effectiveness of your exercises.

Building a Workout Plan

Crafting a personalized workout plan is a crucial step toward achieving your bodybuilding goals. Learn how to design a comprehensive and balanced routine that targets different muscle groups, ensuring holistic development and preventing imbalances.

Nutrition: Fueling Your Transformation

Understand the role of nutrition in bodybuilding and explore essential guidelines for a balanced and effective diet. From macronutrients to meal timing, this chapter provides the nutritional foundation necessary to support your body's growth and recovery.

The Art of Meal Prepping

Unlock the secrets of meal prepping – a practical strategy to ensure you stay on track with your nutrition goals. Discover time-saving tips and delicious recipes that make meal prepping an enjoyable and integral part of your bodybuilding lifestyle.

Chapter 2: The Fundamental Exercises

Embark on a journey through the fundamental exercises that form the cornerstone of any effective bodybuilding routine. Each exercise is meticulously explained, ensuring you not only perform them correctly but also understand their impact on specific muscle groups.

Leg Swing to Cable Crossover Fly: A Comprehensive Guide

From dynamic warm-up exercises like leg swings to targeted muscle-building movements like the cable crossover fly, this chapter covers a diverse range of exercises. Dive into the nuances of each movement, including proper form, common mistakes to avoid, and variations to cater to different fitness levels.

Developing a Strong Foundation: Leg Exercises

Start your bodybuilding journey by strengthening the foundation – your legs. Uncover the secrets behind squats, deadlifts, and various leg isolation exercises. Understanding the mechanics of these exercises not only helps prevent injuries but also ensures optimal muscle engagement for maximum gains.

Sculpting Your Back: Pull-ups to Back Extension

Your back is a canvas waiting to be sculpted. Explore a myriad of back exercises, from bodyweight pull-ups to cable rows, designed to target different areas of your back. Learn the importance of a well-developed back in enhancing overall aesthetics and functional strength.

Building Bolder Shoulders and Arms: Overhead Barbell Press to EZ Bar Preacher Curl

Achieve those coveted boulder shoulders and powerful arms with a comprehensive guide to shoulder and arm exercises. Master the overhead barbell press, dumbbell side raise, and various curl variations to ensure balanced development and a symmetrical physique.

Strengthening Your Core: Dead Hang to Cable Pallof Press

A strong core is the backbone of a powerful physique. Delve into core exercises that go beyond traditional sit-ups, including the dead hang, plank variations, and cable exercises that target your entire midsection. A robust core not only enhances your aesthetic appeal but also improves overall stability and posture.

Mastering Chest Development: Push-ups to Machine Chest Press

Unleash the power of a well-defined chest with a detailed guide to chest exercises. From the foundational push-up to the machine chest press, discover the techniques that maximize chest engagement and promote balanced development.

Flexibility and Recovery: Stretches and Restorative Exercises

While building muscle is crucial, maintaining flexibility and incorporating restorative practices is equally important. Explore stretches and exercises that enhance flexibility, aid recovery, and contribute to long-term joint health. This holistic approach ensures longevity in your bodybuilding journey.

Chapter 3: The 12-Week Jump-Start Program

Having laid the groundwork with foundational knowledge and fundamental exercises, it's time to put theory into practice. The 12-week jump-start program is a meticulously crafted plan that takes you through progressive stages, gradually building strength, endurance, and muscle mass.

Weekly Progression: A Strategic Approach

Each week of the program is designed with specific goals, gradually increasing the intensity to challenge your body and stimulate continuous growth. Understand the rationale behind the progression and how it optimally stimulates muscle adaptation.

Nutritional Guidance During the Program

Nutrition plays a pivotal role during the 12-week program. Explore tailored nutritional guidelines, emphasizing the importance of macronutrients, hydration, and supplementation to support your body's increased demands during this intensive training phase.

Incorporating Periodization: A Key to Sustainable Growth

The 12-week jump-start program employs the principles of periodization, strategically varying the intensity and volume of workouts. Understand how this method prevents plateaus, reduces the risk of overtraining, and promotes sustained progress throughout the program.

Mental Resilience and Mind-Muscle Connection

Embarking on a transformative journey requires mental resilience. Explore techniques to enhance your mental focus and cultivate a strong mind-muscle connection. This connection not only improves the effectiveness of your workouts but also contributes to a more profound mind-body synergy.

Recovery Strategies: Balancing Intensity and Rest

Balancing intense workouts with adequate rest is paramount for growth. Delve into recovery strategies, including proper sleep, active recovery days, and the importance of listening to your body. These practices ensure that your body remains in an optimal state for muscle repair and growth.

Adapting the Program to Your Unique Needs

While the 12-week program provides a structured framework, it's essential to adapt it to your unique needs and circumstances. Learn how to make adjustments based on your progress, personal preferences, and any unforeseen challenges that may arise.

Chapter 4: Conclusion

As you approach the conclusion of this comprehensive guide, reflect on the transformative journey you've embarked upon. This chapter ties together the threads of bodybuilding philosophy, exercise science, nutrition, and the practical application of the 12-week jump-start program.

Celebrating Achievements and Setting New Goals

Take a moment to celebrate the achievements you've made during your bodybuilding journey. From mastering essential techniques to completing the 12-week program, acknowledge the hard work and dedication that brought you to this point. Then, set new goals that propel you toward continued growth and success.

Integrating Bodybuilding into a Lifestyle

Bodybuilding isn't just a temporary endeavor; it's a lifestyle. Explore strategies for integrating the principles of bodybuilding into your daily life, ensuring that the habits you've cultivated during this journey become a sustainable part of your overall well-being.

Inspiring Others and Building a Community

Share your success story and inspire others to embark on their own bodybuilding journey. Building a supportive community enhances motivation, provides valuable insights, and creates a network of individuals dedicated to personal growth and well-being.

The Ever-Evolving Journey: Lifelong Learning in Bodybuilding

Understand that your bodybuilding journey is a lifelong learning process. Embrace the evolution of your goals, techniques, and understanding of your body. This conclusion sets the stage for a continued exploration of the multifaceted world of bodybuilding.

In closing, "The Ultimate Bodybuilding Guide for Beginners" is more than a manual; it's your companion in unlocking your full potential. Whether you're a novice or a seasoned fitness enthusiast, this guide offers a roadmap to sculpting not just your body but a healthier, stronger, and more resilient version of yourself. Embrace the journey, celebrate the milestones, and let the transformative power of bodybuilding unfold before you.

CONTENTS

PART ONE

SETTING THE FOUNDATION

WHEN MOST PEOPLE begin bodybuilding, they make the mistake of jumping into a workout routine that is too advanced. It's a mistake I made early on in my career. No one wants to consider themselves a beginner at something, but if you start out doing too much, it can lead to injuries, burnout, and even hindrances to long-term progress. As a beginner, it's important to develop the proper fundamentals and build a strong foundation. That's why my program is effective, medically sound, and backed by science.

BODYBUILDING

IN THIS SECTION, we dig into the science of bodybuilding and highlight a few important details that will make your bodybuilding experience as successful as possible.

UNDERSTANDING BODYBUILDING SCIENCE

The scientific process behind bodybuilding—and how muscles are built—can best be described in three steps: stimulus, recovery, and adaptation.

The process starts in the gym with a stimulus (workout), which causes micro tears in your muscles. Immediately after the workout, the body's recovery systems begin to heal and rebuild damaged tissue. It's common to hear, "You don't build muscle or gain strength while you are at the gym." As counterintuitive as that sounds, it's true. Muscle size and strength are both reduced immediately after the training session as the body repairs itself. Once recovery occurs, however, so does the desired adaptation, because the stress has sparked additional tissue growth. When bodybuilding is the goal, training results in larger muscles and increased strength. Rest days, proper nutrition, and smart programming are an essential part of that process.

SETTING PERSONAL GOALS

In order to accomplish anything great, you first need to set some meaningful goals. Bodybuilding offers various possibilities based on your personal objectives.

GOAL #1 – BUILD MUSCLE

When people think of bodybuilding, the first thing that usually comes to mind is building muscle, also referred to as muscle hypertrophy. This is the appropriate goal for most beginners and anyone who is underweight. I always tell my clients that focusing on building muscle is investing in your long-term physique development. To build muscle effectively, your training program needs to be combined with a diet that provides a caloric surplus (more calories than you need to maintain your bodyweight).

GOAL #2 – LOSE FAT

Fat loss is an important aspect of bodybuilding that isn't always obvious. In order to have the "bodybuilder look," the fact is that you need a lean physique. A lean physique is more impressive when combined with adequate muscle mass. While most people should prioritize building muscle first, focusing on fat loss first can be a smart decision if you have accumulated too much body fat. To lose fat effectively, your training program needs to be combined with a diet that creates a caloric deficit (fewer calories than you need to maintain your bodyweight).

GOAL #3 – GAIN STRENGTH

Although increased strength is often associated with powerlifting, it's a great way to build your physique. Plus, strength gains can be measured numerically, which makes it easier to track your progress. You can increase absolute strength, muscular endurance, or even relative strength, which is your strength-to-bodyweight ratio.

GOAL #4 – COMPETE

At some point, you may decide to set your sights on competitive bodybuilding, which is a great way to push yourself to the next level. In recent years, the sport has added multiple divisions for both men and women. In addition to traditional bodybuilding, there are Men's Physique and Classic Physique divisions along with Women's Bikini,

Figure, and Physique divisions. There really is a category for everyone!

TRACKING YOUR PROGRESS

Keeping track of your progress is an important part of the process, and seeing changes in your physique is one of the best ways to stay motivated! We will be doing a check-in every three weeks to monitor your progress, starting with Day 1.

Bodyweight

Keeping track of bodyweight is one of the easiest and best ways to monitor progress. The scale doesn't always tell the full story, but it's an invaluable tool. Check your bodyweight first thing in the morning, nude, after going to the bathroom. Due to normal daily fluctuations, a good habit to get into is checking your bodyweight under these conditions multiple times per week and calculating a weekly average.

Pictures

It's been said that "a picture tells a thousand words," and that is certainly the case when it comes to gauging your progress. It's hard to see changes in your physique by looking in the mirror every day. However, when you go back and compare pictures from previous weeks, the progress is much more visible.

Each week, take front, side, and rear photos at the same place in your house with the same amount of lighting, at the same time of the day, and wearing similar clothes. Make sure you take them on Day 1 so you can have an awesome "Before and After" set of photos at the end of the program.

Circumference Measurements

Measuring changes in specific body parts is a great way to analyze muscle mass gains and fat loss. Like tracking bodyweight and taking photos, it's important to be as consistent as possible when measuring the circumferences of the chest, arm, waist, hips/glutes, and thigh.

Body Fat Percentage

Although body fat analysis can be a great way to measure progress, we're not going to use it, simply because most people don't have a reliable way to do it. However, if you have access to a DXA scan, underwater weighing device, Bod Pod, bioelectrical impedance scale, or someone skilled with skin calipers, feel free to add it to the check-ins. It's important to point out that while some of these methods are more accurate than others, none of them are perfect.

FINDING YOUR GYM

When the time comes to decide where you are going to work out, you have a few options depending on your personal preferences, location, and budget. You can buy equipment to work out at home, go the traditional gym route, or look into a private training facility.

Home

The most convenient place to work out is right in the comfort of your own home. This is a great option for those of us who are busy and short on time. The biggest obstacle is price. In the long term, you may save a little cash by not having to pay for a monthly gym membership, but the up-front investment can be expensive.

EQUIPMENT NEEDED

Before heading out to your local sporting goods store, I highly recommend looking at used equipment first. Most of the time, you can find lightly used equipment selling for a fraction of the original price.

This is the basic equipment needed to start a home gym: squat rack, barbell, weight plates, adjustable bench, and a few resistance bands.

Gym

The most popular place to train is at a standard gym. Before you join, most gyms will offer a free week (or at least a free day) so you can check them out. Here are a few things to look for:

Prices: For the most part, a commercial gym will charge between $30 and $60 per month with a discount for a longer commitment.

Equipment: Make sure the gym has the equipment you need and that the equipment is in good working condition.

Location: Find a gym that is convenient, ideally close to your home or work.

Private Training

If you desire more one-on-one attention, working with a trainer in person or online is a great option. Nearly all gyms have personal trainers who can help you with technique, exercise selection, and accountability. Online personal training can also be a more affordable and more flexible way to reap all the benefits of an in-person trainer.

SEMIPRIVATE/GROUP CLASSES

Semiprivate group training has gained a lot of traction in recent years. From a social standpoint, it can be great for accountability if you are motivated to train as part of a group. Group training is also a more affordable way to work with a personal trainer, although it will be more expensive than a regular gym membership.

LEARNING ESSENTIAL TECHNIQUES

To get the most out of your workouts, it's important to understand how to breathe/brace under load, utilize proper form, understand reps/sets, and properly select weights.

Breathing/Bracing

To understand how to properly breathe when lifting weights, it's important to know how to create tension with the Valsalva maneuver. This is a technique for holding your breath while applying pressure with your abdominal and thoracic muscles. It's essentially bracing yourself as if you were going to get punched in the stomach. The tension created by this maneuver allows you to exert the maximum force and prevent injury.

Proper Form

Lifting weights is like any skill that improves with practice, so it's very important to learn the correct form right from the beginning. It's easier to learn how to do something right the first time than to try to go back and fix bad habits.

Reps/Sets

A "rep" is short for repetition and refers to one complete movement of an exercise. For example, squatting down and coming up is one repetition. A series of consecutive reps is known as a "set."

Proper Weight Amounts

Understanding how much weight to use is very important. For the most part, you want to start light and gradually increase the amount of weight as you get stronger. In the beginning, the weights should feel comfortable and be relatively easy to lift. This will help you learn proper technique.

Once you have a feel for how to perform all the exercises, most sets should be carried out close to muscle failure (when you can barely get through the last rep), but reaching actual failure is not necessary.

In order to better understand how much weight to use, you should keep 1 to 3 reps "in the tank" at the end of each set. In other words, finish the set before you experience complete muscle failure.

BUILDING A WORKOUT PLAN

As a beginner, having a well-organized, in-depth plan is very important if you want to see the best results.

Warm-up

Skipping the warm-up is one of many mistakes I made as a novice lifter. Warming up is definitely not "sexy," but it's an essential part of the workout process that can enhance or diminish your ability to perform optimal workouts.

Upper and Lower Body

The workout program will be divided into upper-body and lower-body days to provide a balanced training approach. That allows you to hit all muscle groups twice a week without needing to be in the gym for long training sessions.

Abs

You may have heard the expression "abs are made in the kitchen," but that's only partly true. To have a ripped six-pack, you need to be lean, which absolutely requires a good diet. Abs also need to be trained like any other muscle to be properly developed.

Circuits

In this program, we'll use circuit training, which allows you to get a lot of work done in a short amount of time. Circuits involve doing back-to-back exercises with little rest in between.

Cooldown

In the past, kids used to stretch before gym class or playing a sport. Recent research, however, has shown the limitations of static pre-exercise stretching. It turns out that stretching is most effective at the end of the workout, when the muscles are warm and the body is ready to unwind.

Rest and Recover

To get the most out of your workouts, you need to allow your body to rest and recover. Every week, you'll take three days off from the gym. This doesn't mean you need to be sedentary. I recommend doing some "active recovery," which is a form of light (low-intensity) exercise that can actually enhance recovery from your hard workouts.

Catching Up

Life happens. If something comes up and you have to miss a workout, it's no big deal. All you need to do is reschedule the missed workout on one of the planned rest days.

Preventing Injury

Using proper technique, warming up, and taking rest days will go a long way toward preventing injuries. However, don't ignore aches and pains. If something doesn't feel right or an exercise causes pain, work around it. Don't lean more deeply into it.

CARDIO

Cardio can be an important part of the training program, especially if your main goal is to lose fat.

Most of us live sedentary lives, which means we don't expend many calories. The first action step to a healthier, leaner body is to reverse that trend and increase daily activity. You can do cardio exercise with 20 to 30 minutes on a treadmill or elliptical or take a few 10-minute walks using one of the fitness apps to track your activity.

On the other hand, cardio is less important if your goal is to build muscle. You will get most, if not all, of the cardiovascular health benefits you need just from lifting weights.

NUTRITION

UNDERSTANDING QUALITY nutrition is critical if you want to see results. Eating the right foods at the right times—and in the right amounts—will help you perform better and regulate your bodyweight.

Energy balance (calories in versus calories out) is key when it comes to building muscle and losing fat. When the goal is to build muscle, you need to consume slightly more calories than your body requires to maintain weight. On the other hand, when the goal is to lose fat, you need to eat slightly fewer calories than required.

ESSENTIAL NUTRITIONAL GUIDELINES

When it comes to nutrition, experts will tell you different things. At the end of the day, however, adherence to your diet of choice is what is most important. I refer to this as "nutritional consistency" because the best diet is going to be the one you can stick to long term.

You don't have to drive yourself crazy counting calories, weighing, measuring, and quantifying everything you put in your mouth. First and foremost, you want to develop good nutritional habits.

Calorie Intake

Every discussion of nutrition needs to start with calorie intake. Before we get into the details, we must figure out how many calories your body needs to maintain its weight (maintenance calorie intake).

Step 1 – Baseline Number: Calculate bodyweight by multiplying weight (in pounds) by 10

Example: 165 lbs. x 10 = 1,650

Take the baseline number and use an activity multiplier for your maintenance calorie intake.

Sedentary (fewer than 5,000 steps per day and fewer than 4 workouts per week)

Baseline number x 1.2 to 1.4

Average (between 5,000 and 8,000 steps per day and fewer than 4 workouts per week)

Baseline number x 1.4 to 1.6

Active (more than 8,000 steps per day and at least 4 workouts per week)

Baseline number x 1.6 ≤

Example: 1,650 x 1.5 (average activity) = 2,475

In our example, 2,475 would be the number of calories needed to maintain the bodyweight of a 165-pound individual with an average activity level. You would add 300 to 500 calories per day to gain weight or subtract 300 to 500 calories per day to lose weight.

Protein Intake

To build and maintain muscle, you need to boost muscle protein synthesis and reduce muscle breakdown. The best way to do that is to consume around 1 gram of protein per day per pound of bodyweight.

PROTEIN SHAKES

There is nothing magical about protein shakes other than providing a convenient way to help you meet your daily protein requirements.

Other quality protein sources include eggs, egg whites, chicken breast, white fish, salmon, lean red meat, turkey, lean pork, Greek yogurt, low-fat cottage cheese, low-fat cheese, and low-fat milk. Protein contains 4 calories per gram.

Fat Intake

The word "fat" has a negative connotation, but consuming dietary fat doesn't make you more likely to gain fat. The truth is, some fat is essential, meaning the body needs to consume it to stay alive. Fat plays an important role in regulating hormones, aiding joint health, boosting brain function, and more. Ideally, fat should make up about 20 to 40 percent of your total calorie intake.

Quality fat sources include nuts or nut butter, avocados, olive oil, heavy whipping cream, egg yolks, salmon, and full-fat dairy products.

Fat contains 9 calories per gram.

Carbohydrate Intake

Carbohydrates have gotten a bad rap in recent years. What's actually true is that consuming carbs does not lead to fat gain. Eating a diet too high in *overall calories* leads to fat gain.

SUGAR

There is nothing inherently wrong with sugar, which exists in fruit, milk, and other "healthy" foods. The issue is, most sugary foods are easy to over-consume and are void of nutrients. Aim to focus most of your carbohydrate consumption on nutrient dense, complex carb sources.

Quality carbohydrate sources include oatmeal, rice, rice cakes, potatoes, fruits, vegetables, and whole-grain bread and pasta.

Carbohydrates contain 4 calories per gram.

Pre- and Post-Workout Nutrition

When it comes to pre- and post-workout nutrition, overall calorie and macronutrient intake is what matters most. Still, to maximize performance in the gym, consider optimizing nutrition around your workouts.

Before you exercise, eat something that provides you with enough energy to train but not too much substance to slow you down. This will vary from person to person. I recommend eating a balanced meal or snack containing protein, carbohydrates, and fat about 1 to 3 hours before you work out. When you're done, eat another balanced meal of protein, carbohydrates, and fat as soon as you can.

Note: Most people who are just weightlifting will need only water during their workouts.

HYDRATION

The body does a great job of regulating our fluid intake by adjusting our levels of thirst. Have water or even other drinks such as coffee, tea, milk, and diet soda, etc., available to you all day, and sip as needed.

Here is a list of 20 meals and 10 snack ideas to help with nutritional consistency before and after workouts and throughout the day. Use them as a guide to help you plan your daily menu.

MEALS

1. 4 egg whites, 2 whole eggs, ¾ cup oats, 1 apple
2. 2 whole eggs, 1 cup vanilla Greek yogurt, ½ cup oats
3. 1 scoop protein powder mixed with 1 cup almond milk, 2 slices wheat toast with 2 tablespoons peanut butter
4. 4 egg whites, 4 slices bacon, 1 cup oats
5. 2 whole eggs with 1 slice low-fat cheese, 2 pieces Canadian bacon, 1 bagel with low-fat cream cheese
6. 3 whole eggs, 1 cup cereal with 1 cup low-fat milk
7. 3 egg whites, 2 whole eggs, 1 serving spinach, ¾ cup oats, 1 serving berries
8. 1 chicken breast (4 to 6 ounces), 1 cup rice, 1 serving broccoli, 1 ounce almonds

9. Lean red meat (4 to 6 ounces), 1 sweet potato (8 ounces), 1 cup asparagus

10. Salmon (4 to 6 ounces), 1 russet potato (8 ounces), large green salad with 1 tablespoon low-fat dressing

11. Chicken thighs (6 to 8 ounces), 1 cup brown rice, 1 cup green beans

12. 1 chicken breast (4 to 6 ounces), 1 cup pasta with 1 serving red sauce, 1 cup green peppers/onions

13. Lean ground beef (4 to 6 ounces), 2 whole-grain tortillas, ½ cup rice, ½ cup black beans, lettuce, tomatoes, onions, peppers, etc.

14. 1 pork loin (4 to 6 ounces), 1 cup rice, large green salad with 1 to 2 tablespoons salad dressing

15. 1 can tuna, 1 cup rice with 1 tablespoon butter, ½ cup green beans

16. Shrimp (4 to 6 ounces), 1 cup rice, 1 serving stir-fried vegetables with 1 to 2 tablespoons teriyaki sauce

17. Lean red meat (6 to 8 ounces), 1 russet potato (8 to 10 ounces), large green salad with 1 to 2 tablespoons light salad dressing

18. 1 turkey breast (4 ounces), 2 slices of wheat bread, lettuce, and tomato; 1 low-fat cheese stick; 1 apple; 1 ounce almonds

19. 2 tablespoons peanut butter, 2 tablespoons jelly, and 2 slices of wheat bread; 1 cup vanilla Greek yogurt

20. 1 can tuna, 1 tablespoon light mayo, and 2 slices of wheat bread; 1 serving baby carrots; 1 ounce almonds

SNACKS

1. 1 scoop protein powder, 1 banana, 1 tablespoon peanut butter

2. 1 protein bar

3. 2 ounces beef jerky, 1 apple, 1 ounce almonds

4. ½ cup plain Greek yogurt with 1 scoop protein powder and 1 serving berries

5. 2 flavored rice cakes with 1 to 2 tablespoons peanut butter mixed with 1 scoop protein powder

6. 1 ounce beef jerky, 1 cheese stick, handful of mixed nuts

7. 1 cup cottage cheese with ½ cup pineapple

8. 1 scoop protein powder mixed with 1 cup low-fat milk

9. 1 apple, celery with 2 tablespoons peanut butter

10. 1 cup Greek yogurt, 1 package (about 1½ ounces) peanut butter crackers

SUPPLEMENTS

As a teenager, I wasted a lot of money buying worthless supplements. The truth is that very few supplements live up to their claims. Even those with some research behind them tend to be hit or miss. Here are a few supplements I recommend:

• Protein powder can be used as needed to help reach daily protein goals. There are many different products, including whey concentrate, whey isolate, milk protein isolate, casein, and vegan blends with pea or hemp protein.

• Creatine monohydrate is generally considered to be a safe supplement that can help you build muscle and gain strength. Take 3 to 5 grams daily.

• Caffeine is well known for its ability to help you wake up in the morning, but it has also been shown to improve focus and performance in the gym. Consume 200 to 400 milligrams about 30 minutes before exercising with a cup or two of coffee (about 100 milligrams of caffeine per 8-ounce cup) or a caffeine pill (100 milligrams).

• Fish oil can make up for a lack of omega-3 fatty acids in your diet. Consume 2 to 4 capsules per day with a meal.

• Vitamin D is a fat soluble vitamin that our skin synthesizes when exposed to the sun. Most people do not get enough sunlight or vitamin D in their diets for optimal levels. Take 1,000 to 2,000 IUs of vitamin D_3 per day.

THE ART OF MEAL PREPPING

Meal prepping is routine within the bodybuilding community—and for good reason! Cooking your food ahead of time is one of the best ways to ensure you stay on your diet for the long haul. It also saves you time and money. Here are a few tips to help you master the art of meal prepping.

Kitchen Tips

Plan out your meals ahead of time. Before you go to the store, write down what you intend to cook for the week, including breakfasts, lunches, dinners, and snacks, and make a complete shopping list of what you need.

Buy in bulk. You'll notice you end up eating a lot of the same foods. Core bodybuilding items like chicken breasts, eggs, oatmeal, and rice are cheaper when you buy them in bulk.

Cook twice per week. Food doesn't taste good after a few days in the refrigerator, so cook your meals twice a week. Sundays and Wednesdays seem to work well for a lot of people.

Invest in quality storage containers. I personally like to use glass containers, but plastic works as well. Make sure you buy well-made ones that will stand up to frequent use and washing.

Keep a lot of spices and sauces on hand. Food doesn't have to be bland to be nutritious. Feel free to add flavorful spices and low-calorie sauces to your meals.

Buy a slow cooker. A slow cooker is a bodybuilder's best friend. You can literally set it and forget it.

PART TWO
THE FUNDAMENTAL EXERCISES

BEFORE YOU START training, it's important that you know exactly how to perform the exercises. Pay attention to the details such as foot placement and hand grip, which can play a big role in getting the most out of each workout.

Everyone's body is unique; our limbs are different, and our biomechanics vary. Remember that proper form may look a little different for you compared to that of your workout partner. Use the information in this section as a starting point and you'll find what works best for you.

LEGS AND GLUTES

Leg Swing
Air Squat
Back Squat
Deadlift
Romanian Deadlift
Dumbbell Step-up
Dumbbell Bulgarian Split Squat
Barbell Hip Thrust
Leg Press
Leg Extension
Seated Leg Curl
Seated Calf Raise
Couch Stretch
Hurdle Stretch

Many people neglect lower-body training when they first start working out. I get it. It's more appealing to focus on beach muscles like the chest, biceps, and abs. Skipping Leg Day has become a meme in today's gym culture in a nod to bodybuilders who prioritize upper-body aesthetics, but it's a big mistake. Bodybuilding is all about symmetry. Nothing looks more ridiculous than someone with a huge upper body supported by toothpick legs.

From a functional standpoint, legs are the foundation of the body. All human movement starts with the legs—walking, running, jumping, balancing, turning, lifting boxes, carrying your kids . . . The list goes on. A strong lower body can improve how you perform nearly all of your day-to-day activities. Research has even shown a close association between leg strength and longevity!

The legs and gluteal muscles (glutes) are big muscles that need heavy weights to be trained effectively. Because of this, lower-body workouts often require more effort and produce more fatigue than upper-body workouts. Don't let this discourage you. Embrace the challenge and know you are one of the few people in the gym benefiting from taking lower-body training seriously.

LEG SWING

PRIMARY MUSCLES: QUADRICEPS, HAMSTRINGS, GLUTES, AND HIPS

Leg swings are a dynamic warm-up exercise that prepares the lower body for physical activity. Unlike static stretches where you hold one stationary position, dynamic stretches allow you to move through a range of motion. This not only reduces risk of injury, but it also can help improve performance.

INSTRUCTIONS

1. Stand with your feet shoulder-width apart and extend your arms against a wall or a sturdy object. Leave enough room to swing your legs in front of you.

2. With your arms extended, stand on your left leg. Extend your right leg to the side so that it is just off the ground.

3. Begin by swinging the right leg to the outside as far as you can and then swinging it back toward your body, crossing the left leg, as far as you can. This completes one rep. Finish the set (the number of reps depends on where you are in the 12-week program), and then repeat on the other side.

Common Mistakes and How to Avoid Them

Mistake: Opening up your hips

Avoid opening up your hips when swinging your leg out to the side. Keep your core tight and hips square throughout the entire exercise.

 GENERAL TIP

Keep your legs loose. Shake out any tension below your hips.

Front and back leg swings– This option involves swinging your legs from front to back instead of (or in addition to) swinging them from side to side.

AIR SQUAT

PRIMARY MUSCLES: QUADRICEPS, HAMSTRINGS, AND GLUTES

The air squat is an exercise that not only reinforces the squat movement pattern but also gets the lower body warmed up and ready to perform. It's a good habit to do an air squat before any type of loaded squat exercise.

INSTRUCTIONS

1. Start in a standing position with your feet roughly shoulder-width apart.
2. Drop your hips back like you are sitting in a chair while simultaneously bending your knees. Continue moving down until your hips are below the tops of your knees.
3. Once you reach your lowest point, stand up. To help with balance, extend your arms directly in front of you as you move.

Common Mistakes and How to Avoid Them

Mistake: Leaning too far forward

Try to keep your torso as vertical as possible. Avoid bending forward at the waist during the exercise.

 GENERAL TIP

Start each day with 5 to 10 air squats in the morning. It's not only a great warm-up for a lower body workout; it's also a great warm-up for the day.

CHANGE IT UP

The box air squat–This exercise alternative involves lowering yourself onto a box or bench that allows your knees to bend at a 90-angle degree.

BACK SQUAT

PRIMARY MUSCLES: QUADRICEPS, HAMSTRINGS, AND GLUTES

The back squat, referred to as the "king of all exercises," is one of the fundamental movements in bodybuilding. It uses nearly the entire muscle system while developing the lower body in ways unlike any other exercise. If I could pick only one movement for this training program, the back squat would be the one.

INSTRUCTIONS

Phase 1: The Setup

1. Start with the barbell resting in a stand at about chest level.
2. Grab the bar with a tight grip that's slightly wider than shoulder width.
3. Step under the bar and position your feet parallel to each other.
4. Squeeze your shoulder blades together to create a "shelf" for the bar to rest on. Place the bar in a balanced position across your upper back and shoulders.
5. Once the bar is set, take a deep breath, brace your core, and extend your hips and knees to lift the bar out of the rack.
6. After you remove the barbell from the stand, take two short and deliberate steps straight back. Your feet should end up slightly wider than shoulder-width apart. Most people benefit from pointing their toes slightly out. This is the starting position for each rep.

Phase 2: The Squat

1. Once you are in the starting position, take a deep breath, brace your core, and begin the descent.
2. Bend at the knees while dropping your hips back until the tops of your thighs are parallel to the ground.
3. The moment they are parallel, stand back up to the starting position.

Common Mistakes and How to Avoid Them

Mistake: Knees caving in

Knee cave while squatting is a common mistake. If your knees move toward each other as you stand up from the squat, it can potentially lead to knee pain or injury over time. There are two things you can do to avoid this problem:

Move your feet closer together. If the starting foot position is too wide, the body will compensate by moving the knees toward each other. Try tightening your stance closer to shoulder-width position. Drive your knees out. A common coaching cue to help improve knee tracking is simply to focus on driving the knees out during the lift. Sometimes just being mindful of knee position helps take care of the problem.

✚ GENERAL TIP

Unlike most lifting exercises, the type of shoes you wear when squatting is important. Ideally, you want something with a hard, flat surface. Converse Chuck Taylors or most Vans shoes fit the bill. Another option is to use an Olympic weightlifting shoe, which is specifically designed for squatting. This shoe has an elevated heel that can help you maintain an upright posture while squatting at or below parallel. Most important, you want to avoid squatting in running shoes. The soft soles in most running shoes will make you feel as if you are trying to squat on a pillow. Running shoes are great for running but not for squatting.

Goblet squat–If you are not comfortable using a barbell yet, you can still take advantage of the movement's benefits by doing a goblet squat variation. Instead of placing a barbell on your back, hold a dumbbell or kettlebell out in front of you.

Front squat–For an advanced variation, try a front squat. A front squat shifts more focus onto the quadriceps and also requires more upper-back strength as well! This variation is simply a squat with the barbell placed across the front of your shoulders.

DEADLIFT

PRIMARY MUSCLES: HAMSTRINGS, GLUTES, AND BACK

Like the squat, the deadlift is one of the foundational exercises in bodybuilding. In fact, some fitness professionals say the deadlift is a more effective total-body exercise than the squat. Regardless, the deadlift is a great exercise to build muscle and strength along the entire posterior chain (back, hamstrings, and glutes). The deadlift is also one of the most functional exercises you can do in the gym.

INSTRUCTIONS

1. Stand facing a barbell with your feet about shoulder-width apart. Your shins should be a couple of inches away from the bar. (In other words, the bar should appear to cut your feet in half.)

2. Squat down to grab the bar while keeping your hips lower than your shoulders. Your hands should be outside of your knees, and your elbows should be fully extended. Your arms stay locked out throughout the entire movement.

3. When you grab the bar, your back should be flat or slightly arched, and your hips should be above parallel, creating tension in the hamstrings. This is the starting position.

4. Take a deep breath, brace your core, and lift the bar from the floor by extending your hips and knees.

5. Your torso angle should remain constant. Avoid letting your hips rise before your shoulders. Your back should remain flat.

6. As the bar is being raised, keep it as close to your body as possible.

7. Once the bar passes your knees, drive your hips forward and extend your legs. Finish standing straight up with your shoulders behind the bar.

8. With a straight back, return the bar to the starting position.

Common Mistakes and How to Avoid Them

Mistake: Rounding your back

The biggest deadlifting mistake is allowing the back to round. This can be caused by multiple factors, but I think the biggest reason is a lack of tension on the bar before starting the lift.

Before even lifting the weight off the ground, it's important to create that tension. Some coaches like to call this "taking the slack out." Once you're in the starting position, pull the bar up only enough to apply upward pressure but not enough to actually lift the weight off the ground. This should be maybe 5 to 10 percent of the force necessary to actually lift the weight. This helps get your muscles activated and ready before they need to actually lift the weight. It also prevents your hips from shooting up early and causing the back to round.

 GENERAL TIP

If you find it hard to hang on to the bar during the lift, you can use what is called a "mixed grip" to prevent the bar from rolling out of your hands. To use a mixed grip, place one hand over the bar (pronated), but reverse the grip with the other hand and grab the bar underhand (supinated).

CHANGE IT UP

Trap bar deadlift–The traditional barbell deadlift can be difficult to master when first starting out. A great alternative is a trap bar deadlift. The movement pattern is nearly the same, but the handles are at your sides so it allows you to get in a better starting position.

Sumo deadlift–There are two deadlift variations: conventional and sumo. We focus on conventional deadlifts in this book because those are the easiest to learn. Once you master the conventional deadlift, you can experiment with the sumo stance, where foot placement is about twice as wide as your shoulders and hand placement is inside of your legs.

ROMANIAN DEADLIFT

PRIMARY MUSCLES: HAMSTRINGS, GLUTES, AND BACK

The Romanian deadlift (RDL) is a deadlift variation that places more emphasis on the hamstrings than a traditional deadlift does. The RDL is one of the best hamstring exercises you can perform. Due to the nature of the exercise, however, it causes significant muscle soreness. Don't be surprised if your hamstrings really ache the day after doing these for the first time!

INSTRUCTIONS

1. Unlike a traditional deadlift, the Romanian deadlift starts with the barbell in a rack just above your knees.

2. Stand with your feet about shoulder-width apart, grab the bar with an overhand or mixed grip (see here), brace the core, and lift the bar out of the rack by extending your knees. From there, take a step back. This is the starting position.

3. Brace your core again, and begin the exercise by hinging at your hips. While hinging, bend forward and push your hips back as the bar slides down your thighs. Maintain a slight bend in your knees during the movement.

4. Once the bar is lowered to the mid-shins, reverse the movement by driving your hips forward and extending your torso back to the starting position.

Common Mistakes and How to Avoid Them

Mistake: Bending your knees too much

Avoid turning this exercise into a regular deadlift. Maintain only a slight bend in the knees and keep the hips high throughout the entire movement. If you feel the need to bend the knees deeper, chances are you are using too much weight.

 GENERAL TIP

With the Romanian deadlift, you want to focus more on getting a good stretch in the hamstrings and less on seeing how much weight you can lift.

CHANGE IT UP

Dumbbell Romanian deadlift–You can use dumbbells in place of the barbell if you choose.

Single-leg dumbbell Romanian deadlift–For an advanced variation, the dumbbell RDL also can be done one leg at a time.

DUMBBELL STEP-UP

PRIMARY MUSCLES: QUADRICEPS, HAMSTRINGS, AND GLUTES

The dumbbell step-up is a great lower-body exercise that develops muscle, strength, and balance. Use a box that measures 12 to 18 inches (30 to 46 centimeters) high or is high enough to create roughly a 90-degree angle at the knee joint when a foot is on the box.

INSTRUCTIONS

1. Hold the dumbbells at your sides while standing about 1 foot away from the box.
2. Raise one leg to place your entire foot on the box.
3. As you step onto the box, keep your torso erect and avoid leaning forward. Push off with the lead leg already on the box and bring your back foot onto the box.
4. Once both feet are on the box, pause for a second before returning both feet to the ground, one leg at a time.
5. Repeat with the other leg.

Common Mistakes and How to Avoid Them

Mistake: Using too much weight

The biggest mistake with a dumbbell step-up is using too much weight.

This causes you to lean forward on the way up and puts the lower back in a compromised position. Start light and only add weight that you can lift correctly.

If your grip starts to fail, use a little lifting chalk or even lifting straps to assist you.

Bodyweight step-ups—If using weight is too difficult at first, start with just bodyweight. The exercise is performed the same way, only without holding dumbbells.

Dumbbell lunges—Dumbbell lunges are a great alternative exercise if you do not have a box available.

DUMBBELL BULGARIAN SPLIT SQUAT

PRIMARY MUSCLES: QUADRICEPS, HAMSTRINGS, AND GLUTES

The dumbbell Bulgarian split squat (BSS) is another single-leg exercise that is a great lower-body developer. The BSS is particularly safe and commonly used as a replacement for the back squat if people have a lower-back injury or another limitation.

INSTRUCTIONS

1. Hold two dumbbells (one at each side) while standing in front of a bench.
2. Extend one leg behind you, and rest the top of your foot on the bench.
3. Brace your core, and slowly descend until your back knee is a couple of inches from the ground or your front thigh is parallel to the ground.
4. Extend your knees and hips to return to the starting position. Make sure your torso remains upright during the entire rep, and use controlled movements.
5. Repeat with the other leg.

Common Mistakes and How to Avoid Them

Mistake: Standing too far away or too close to the bench
Determining how far to stand in front of the bench depends on the individual and will take some trial and error to get right. If you stand too far away from the bench, it will be hard to keep the torso upright,

and it may cause pain in the hip area. If you stand too close to the bench, your knee will track too far forward, and it could cause some knee pain. The perfect spot is somewhere in the middle.

 GENERAL TIP

If your gym has a lying leg curl machine, you can place your back foot on the leg pad instead of a bench. Since the lying leg curl pad rolls, it makes the movement a little more comfortable.

 CHANGE IT UP

Bodyweight Bulgarian split squat–If weighted split squats are too difficult at first, feel free to use just your bodyweight.

Barbell Bulgarian split squat– Instead of dumbbells, you can use a barbell on Bulgarian split squats. The exercise is performed the same way, except with a barbell in the back squat position.

BARBELL HIP THRUST

PRIMARY MUSCLES: GLUTES

The barbell hip thrust is the best glute-building exercise there is. If you want to maximize glute development, including the barbell hip thrust is a must. Besides providing aesthetic benefits, glute strength plays a role in many athletic skills, including running and jumping.

INSTRUCTIONS

1. Lean your upper back on a bench with a barbell laying across your hips. Hold the barbell in place with both hands. Keep your feet planted firmly on the ground in front of you about shoulder-width apart. This is the starting position.

2. To begin, drive your hips up toward the sky, engaging your glutes at the top. Perform the movement slowly and with control. It involves a small range of motion, so make sure you raise your hips as high as you can.

3. Once you reach full extension, hold for one count, then lower back to the starting position.

Common Mistakes and How to Avoid Them

Mistake: Not using a full range of motion

Since the barbell hip thrust has a limited range of motion to begin with, it's important to fully extend your hips at the top and use the maximum range. The glutes are most activated at the top of the rep, so you don't want to limit the effectiveness of the exercise.

 GENERAL TIP

You can use a pad or wrap a towel around the barbell to prevent it from digging into your hips when you thrust.

Bodyweight glute bridge– A bodyweight variation can be done by simply lying on your back, with your knees bent, and feet planted on the ground. Drive your hips up and engage your glutes.

Single-leg barbell hip thrust– For a more challenging variation, you can do the barbell hip thrust one leg at a time.

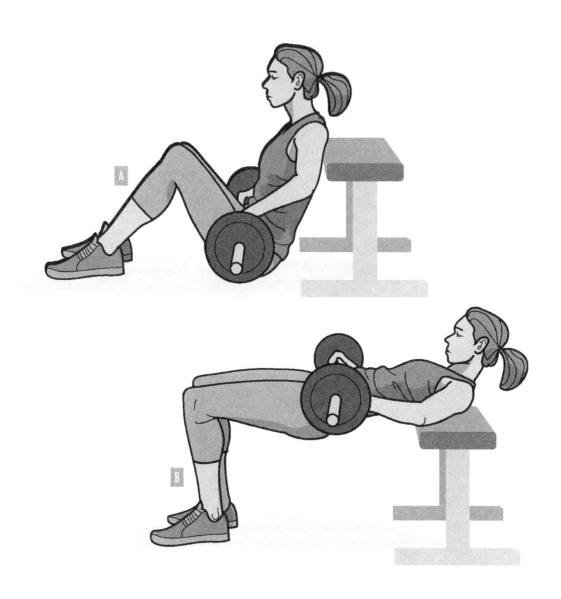

LEG PRESS

PRIMARY MUSCLES: QUADRICEPS, HAMSTRINGS, AND GLUTES

The leg press often is considered an inferior movement to the squat, but that doesn't mean the leg press is not effective. In fact, the leg press is an excellent lower-body movement that requires less skill, and that means a shorter learning curve.

INSTRUCTIONS

1. Position yourself on the leg press machine with your back properly against the backrest and your feet slightly wider than shoulder-width apart on the platform.

2. Grasp the handles at the sides of the machine and release the safety bars.

3. Take a deep breath, brace your core, and bend your knees to start the movement. Bring your knees toward your body so that the thighs nearly touch the torso.

4. With your thighs nearing your torso, reverse the movement by extending your legs back to the starting position without locking your knees.

Common Mistakes and How to Avoid Them

Mistake: Rounding your lower back at the bottom position

Overall, the leg press is a safe and easy exercise, but use caution at the bottom of the movement. If your lower back starts to round when your knees are close to your torso, shorten the range of motion a little bit. As soon as you feel your lower back come off the back pad, return to the starting position. Please note: This is not an excuse to do half reps. You always want to do the biggest range of motion you can safely do.

 GENERAL TIP

By changing where you place your feet on the platform, you can shift the focus of the exercise. Placing your feet low against the foot plate and/or taking a narrow stance shifts more focus onto the quadriceps. Placing your feet higher on the foot plate shifts more focus to the glutes and hamstrings, and placing your feet wider emphasizes the adductors.

CHANGE IT UP

Goblet squat–If your gym doesn't have a leg press, you can replace it with a goblet squat, which involves holding a dumbbell or kettlebell in front of you during the squat movement.

Single-leg press–If you want to focus on one leg at a time, doing a leg press with a single leg is a great variation. Everything is the same, except you put only one foot on the platform at a time.

LEG EXTENSION

PRIMARY MUSCLES: QUADRICEPS

The leg extension provides a great way to isolate the quadriceps muscles in a single-joint exercise. This is a great movement for beginners to develop strength because it doesn't take long to master. Despite what you may have read, the leg extension is a very safe exercise. In fact, it's one of the most common exercises used in rehabilitation.

INSTRUCTIONS

1. Sit on the leg extension machine so the pad supports your back, and grasp the handles along the sides of the seat.

2. Place your feet underneath the bottom roller so it touches the front of your shin and ankle.

3. Contract your quadriceps as you raise your legs to horizontal, stopping just short of locking your knees.

4. Slowly lower your legs in a controlled motion back to the starting position.

Common Mistakes and How to Avoid Them

Mistake: Hips coming off the pad

One mistake people make with the leg extension is allowing their hips to lift off the pad. You want to keep your butt, hips, and lower back area in contact with the pad at all times. One easy way to correct this issue is to pull hard on the side handles and hold yourself in position.

On the last rep of the set, resist the weight for as long as you can on the way down.

Single-leg leg extension—Like with the leg press, if you want to focus on one leg at a time, doing a single-leg leg extension is a great variation. Everything is the same, except you put only one foot under the pad at a time.

Hack squat machine—If your gym has a hack squat machine, a close-stance hack squat is an excellent alternative quad-building exercise. Position your shoulders and back against the pads with your feet slightly closer than shoulder-width apart. Extend your legs to release the safety handles and slowly lower the weight by squatting down until your thighs are at about 90 degrees.

SEATED LEG CURL

PRIMARY MUSCLES: HAMSTRINGS

The seated leg curl provides a great way to isolate the hamstring muscles in a single-joint exercise. This is a relatively easy movement for beginners to develop strength. One of my favorite things about the seated leg curl is how difficult it is to shortcut or "cheat" the exercise by not using a full range of motion, because the machine effectively locks you in place.

INSTRUCTIONS

1. Sit on a leg curl machine, with your legs extended, ankles resting on the ankle pad, and thighs positioned between the thigh pad and the seat. Hold the side handles.
2. Contract your hamstrings and draw your lower legs back toward the seat.
3. Once you have reached the full range of motion, slowly raise your legs back to the starting position.

Common Mistakes and How to Avoid Them

Mistake: Not using a full range of motion

A common mistake is not using a full range of motion, which shortcuts the exercise. As the lower leg gets closer to the seat, the movement gets increasingly harder. Make sure you bring your lower legs as close to the seat as possible in order to get the full benefit from the exercise.

 GENERAL TIP

Holding the ending position (lower leg near the seat) for a second or two before returning to the starting position can make this exercise more effective.

Lying leg curl–To do this option, lie facedown on a lying leg curl machine. Hold the handles with your legs extended and ankles positioned under the ankle pads. Contract your hamstrings to bring your feet toward your glutes. Slowly lower your legs back to the starting position.

SEATED CALF RAISE

PRIMARY MUSCLES: CALVES

The seated calf raise is one of the best exercises to develop both of the calf's muscles: the gastrocnemius, a large muscle that forms the visible bulge in your calf, and the smaller soleus. It's also safe and very easy to do.

INSTRUCTIONS

1. Sit at the calf raise machine with your thighs positioned under the pads and the balls of your feet flat on the foot bar. Make sure your toes are pointed straight ahead.

2. Push up on your toes, and remove the support lever.

3. Relax your ankles, allowing your heels to drop below the step. This is the starting position.

4. Extend your feet and point your toes, raising your heels as high as possible and flexing the calves.

5. Slowly return to the starting position.

Common Mistakes and How to Avoid Them

Mistake: Going too fast

It's easy to get into the habit of doing short, choppy, and fast reps with this exercise. Really slow the movement down and make sure you are using a full range of motion. Get a full stretch at the bottom and come to a full extension at the top. Think about it: Our calves do a bunch of mini-calf raises all day when we walk around, so we need to load and stretch them in new ways.

 GENERAL TIP

To get more out of the exercise, pause between each rep for a couple of seconds when the calves are fully stretched.

CHANGE IT UP

Bodyweight calf raise—You can train your calves with just your bodyweight. Use one hand to balance against a sturdy object, and do calf raises while standing. This can actually get pretty challenging if you go slowly and fully extend at the top.

Standing dumbbell calf raise—This is an option if your gym doesn't have a seated calf raise machine or if you just want a change of pace. Hold a dumbbell in each hand and raise your heels as high as possible while pointing your toes. If balance is an issue, you can do one leg at a time, holding a dumbbell in one hand and using the other to brace yourself against a wall or some kind of support.

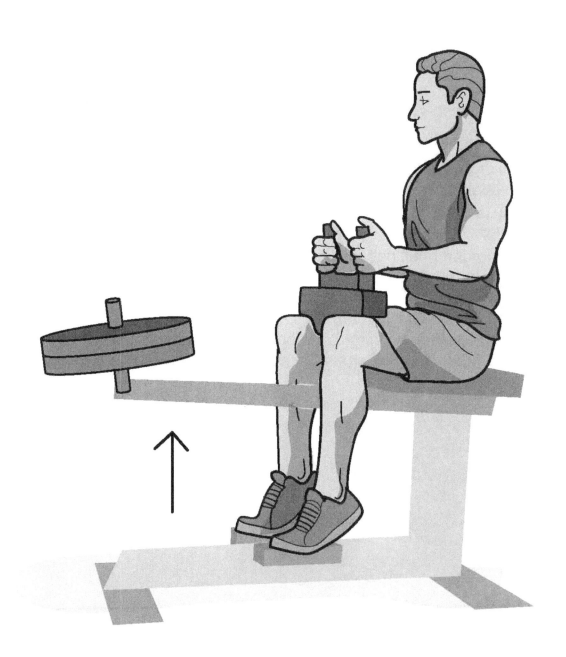

COUCH STRETCH

PRIMARY MUSCLES: QUADRICEPS, HAMSTRINGS, GLUTES, AND HIPS

The couch stretch is a great movement to stretch the quads and hip flexors. This is a stretch that you can do on rest days, too, if your legs or hips are tight.

INSTRUCTIONS

1. To do the couch stretch, you need a bench. Begin the movement by getting into the same position as the end position of the Dumbbell Bulgarian Split Squat, except that you want the back of your knee to touch the ground.

2. Your knee should be in a straight line with the front edge of the bench. Initiate the stretch by pressing your hip forward. Repeat on the other side.

Common Mistakes and How to Avoid Them

Mistake: Rounding your lower back

Keep your rib cage down and core tight while performing the stretch. Avoid rounding your lower back.

 GENERAL TIP

This stretch got its name because you also can use a couch instead of a bench.

CHANGE IT UP

Frog stretch—If your hips are tight and the couch stretch is not hitting the correct area, performing a frog stretch is a great way to open them. Begin by getting down on all fours with your forearms in a plank position. Spread your knees out to the side as far as you can, turning your toes out. Lean back to sit between your ankles.

HURDLE STRETCH

PRIMARY MUSCLES: QUADRICEPS, HAMSTRINGS, GLUTES, AND HIPS

The hurdle stretch has been a standard exercise in physical education classes for years because of its ability to stretch the hamstrings and hip flexors. However, many gym teachers get the timing wrong: This stretch is best done after exercise, not before.

INSTRUCTIONS

1. To perform a hurdle stretch, get into a seated position on the floor and extend one knee at a 45-degree angle from your hips.

2. Position the other leg straight out in front of you. Reach along the straight leg as far as you can and hold. Repeat with the other leg.

Common Mistakes and How to Avoid Them

Mistake: Bending your knee

Don't cheat by bending your knee. Keep the extended leg as straight as possible.

 GENERAL TIP

Each week, aim to stretch a little further.

CHANGE IT UP

Sit and reach–If the hurdle position is uncomfortable, you can sit with both of your legs extended in front of you and lean forward to stretch.

BACK

Rope Lat Extension
Lat Pulldown
Dumbbell Row
Dumbbell Incline Prone Row
Pull-up (Bodyweight, Weighted, Assisted)
Barbell Row
Seated Cable Row
Neutral-Grip Lat Pulldown
Chest-Supported Row
Single-Arm Lat Pulldown
Back Extension
Lat Stretch

The back may be the most underrated muscle group when it comes to beginning bodybuilding. In fact, it's common for back training to be an afterthought altogether. I think this is because the back is not seen as a "show muscle" like the chest, shoulders, and arms. Back development, however, plays a large role when it comes to giving you an impressive physique. A muscular, broad back not only makes you look thick and powerful but it also gives the illusion of a smaller waist. From a performance perspective, the back is one of the few muscle groups that come into play in all three of the big compound exercises—squats, bench presses, and deadlifts. The bottom line is that if you want to lift heavy weights, you need a strong back.

When I talk about back training, I'm referring to the group of muscles that make up the musculature of the back. To train this area, you'll use two main movement patterns: pulldowns and rows.

ROPE LAT EXTENSION

PRIMARY MUSCLES: LATISSIMUS DORSI (LATS)

The rope lat extension is a great exercise to help engage the lats (latissimus dorsi muscles) before a workout. One of the major benefits of this exercise is that, unlike pulldowns or rows, the biceps aren't involved and can't be used to help compensate. This can be helpful for people who have trouble "feeling" their backs work.

INSTRUCTIONS

1. Attach a rope to a high cable pulley, and stand a couple of feet away from the weight stack.
2. With your feet shoulder-width apart, grasp the rope with both hands and lean forward from the hips. Extend your arms up and in front of you. This is the starting position.
3. Keeping your arms straight, pull the rope down toward your thighs. Your hands should end up next to your hips.
4. Return the rope back to the starting position in a controlled manner.

Common Mistakes and How to Avoid Them

Mistake: Turning the exercise into a triceps pressdown

Although lat extensions and triceps pressdowns look very similar from a distance, arm angles are the key difference. With lat extensions, it's very important not to change your elbow angle during the lift. Once you get into position, lock your arms so that they are nearly straight and keep them in that position throughout the movement. You may still feel it in your triceps a little bit, but not nearly as much if you were to allow your elbows to bend during the lift.

 GENERAL TIP

The rope attachment should be set up so that is higher than your head.

🔀 CHANGE IT UP

Straight-bar lat extension– I prefer rope, but the straight bar is a good substitute if rope is not available.

LAT PULLDOWN

PRIMARY MUSCLES: LATISSIMUS DORSI (LATS)

The lat pulldown is a foundational back-building exercise—and for good reason. While nearly all gyms have lat pulldown machines, many people do this easy exercise incorrectly.

INSTRUCTIONS

1. Sit facing the lat pulldown machine with your legs positioned under the pads. Grip the bar with an overhand grip that is slightly wider than shoulder width.
2. Slightly arch your back while pulling the bar down and toward the upper chest.
3. Once the bar comes within an inch or two of your upper chest, slowly return to the starting position.

Common Mistakes and How to Avoid Them

Mistake: Leaning back too far

Leaning back too far is a big mistake, and one that I've seen over and over again. Do not turn this exercise into a rowing movement. Aim to maintain as vertical a torso angle as possible while having a slight back arch and pulling the bar down to your upper chest.

 GENERAL TIP

If you feel your biceps are being overused and you can't feel enough of the workout in your back, try using what's called a "false grip" by not wrapping your thumb around the bar. Think of your hands as hooks and drive down with your elbows.

Extra-wide-grip or narrow-grip lat pulldown–The lat pulldown offers almost endless possibilities for variation. You can change your grip from wide to narrow, overhand to underhand, two-handed to one-handed, and you can even change the bar.

Pull-up–If you don't have access to a lat pulldown machine, you can substitute pull-ups (see here).

DUMBBELL ROW

PRIMARY MUSCLES: LATISSIMUS DORSI (LATS), TERES MAJOR, AND RHOMBOIDS

The dumbbell row is one of the best exercises to build upper-back and lats strength. All you need is a dumbbell and a bench. I really like the dumbbell row because it allows you to work each side separately. Also, because of the unilateral nature of the exercise, you can brace your upper body with one hand while rowing with the other. Being able to brace yourself takes some of the pressure off the lower back.

INSTRUCTIONS

1. Kneeling on the bench, grab a dumbbell with your palm facing in toward your body. Use the opposite hand and a knee on the bench for support.

2. Keeping your back straight, pull the dumbbell up and back toward your hip. Try to get the dumbbell as high as possible.

3. At the top of the movement, allow your shoulder blades to move and retract in order to get the full range of motion.

4. Repeat on the other side.

Common Mistakes and How to Avoid Them

Mistake: Too much torso rotation

People tend to rotate their torsos during the movement because it makes them feel like they're going through a full range of motion. In reality, torso rotation limits lat activation. Keep your shoulders and torso square during the entire exercise. Only the arm and shoulder blade should move.

 GENERAL TIP

This exercise should be done slowly in a controlled way through a full range of motion. It's common for people to use too much weight and end up using every muscle except the back to move the dumbbell. Remember, no one receives a trophy for being the strongest dumbbell rower. Use a weight you can handle. Pause the dumbbell at the top of the motion for a second or two to make the exercise harder and to maximize the muscle contraction.

🔀 CHANGE IT UP

Single-arm seated cable row–For unilateral movement, the single-arm seated cable row is a great variation for dumbbell rows (see here).

Hammer Strength machine iso row–The Hammer Strength iso row machine also provides an amazing single-arm rowing option. This is one of my favorite rowing machines. Sit on the machine, grasp the handles with a neutral or overhand grip, and pull toward your torso.

DUMBBELL INCLINE PRONE ROW

PRIMARY MUSCLES: LATISSIMUS DORSI (LATS), TERES MAJOR, AND RHOMBOIDS

This is one of my top back-building exercises. It's easy to set up and takes almost all the momentum out of the movement, which forces your upper back to move the weight. Also, the support of the incline bench helps to take some pressure off the lower back.

INSTRUCTIONS

1. Start by setting up an adjustable bench at about a 30-degree angle. You'll also want to use a low incline setting of less than 45 degrees.

2. Place two dumbbells on the floor, one on each side of the bench. Lean into the incline bench while reaching for the dumbbells and hold one in each hand.

3. Begin the movement with straight arms.

4. Retract your shoulder blades and row the dumbbells to your side.

5. Pause at the top of the motion, then return to the starting position.

Common Mistakes and How to Avoid Them

Mistake: Using too high of an incline

Ideally, you want to use the lowest incline possible that gives you a full range of motion. If the incline is too high, it takes some tension off your upper back, which you don't want to do.

GENERAL TIP

To make this exercise more effective, try to retract your shoulder blades at the top of the motion as much as possible. When I do it, I picture myself trying to hold a pencil in the middle of my back.

CHANGE IT UP

Seal row–Take advantage of it if your gym has a seal row setup, which is essentially an elevated bench that allows you to row while lying horizontal. This is an excellent exercise, but it can be difficult without the right equipment.

Chest-supported row machine– Any chest-supported row is a good substitute for the dumbbell incline prone row. Most gyms have several different chest-supported row machines, and you can experiment to find the ones that work best for you. Sit on the machine, grasp the handles with a neutral or overhand grip, and pull toward your torso.

PULL-UP (BODYWEIGHT, WEIGHTED, ASSISTED).

PRIMARY MUSCLES: LATISSIMUS DORSI (LATS)

If I had to pick only one back exercise to do for the rest of my life, I would pick the pull-up. The pull-up is one of the most effective lat-building exercises you can do, and the best part is that all you need is a bar to hang from! Pull-ups can be done with bodyweight, weighted, or with added assistance, depending on your strength level.

INSTRUCTIONS

1. Hang from a fixed overhead bar with a wide overhand grip.
2. Pull yourself up so your chin goes over the bar.
3. Drop slowly to the starting position. Your arms should be straight before beginning another rep.

Common Mistakes and How to Avoid Them

Mistake: Not using a full range of motion

The biggest mistake is cutting the rep short, at the beginning or the end. Make sure you pull yourself all the way up so that your chin gets above the bar. At the bottom, start each rep with your arms straight.

 GENERAL TIP

The pull-up is versatile, and I recommend trying multiple grips—wide, close, and neutral. Use an underhand grip if you want to shift a little more emphasis onto the biceps.

Assisted pull-up—The only downside to pull-ups is their difficulty. If you struggle with bodyweight pull-ups, don't be afraid to do assisted pull-ups with a pull-up band. Or you can use an assisted pull-up machine.

Weighted pull-up—On the other hand, if you are great at pull-ups, you can increase intensity by adding extra weight with a weight lifting belt.

BARBELL ROW

PRIMARY MUSCLES: LATISSIMUS DORSI, TERES MAJOR, AND RHOMBOIDS

There is no denying the benefits of the barbell row, which is an essential back-building movement. The biggest upside is the fact that you can handle more weight on a barbell row than on any other row variation.

INSTRUCTIONS

1. Stand with your legs slightly bent and shoulder-width apart. Hold the bar with an overhand grip. Your hands should be slightly wider than shoulder-width apart.

2. Lift the bar out of the rack. Extend your arms, and lean forward 45 degrees at the waist so the bar hangs around your knees. This is the starting position.

3. Pull the bar toward your torso. Keep your torso locked in place, and avoid jerking the bar up as you pull.

4. Touch the bar to your lower abdomen, then slowly drop it to the starting position.

Common Mistakes and How to Avoid Them

Mistake: Turning it into a full-body movement

The biggest mistake with a barbell row is using your full body to lift the weight. The goal with this exercise is to build muscle in the upper back and lat region, not to see how much weight you can throw around with sloppy form. During the movement, keep the torso

89

rigid and the knees slightly bent. Don't allow your back or knee angle to change as you row the barbell up.

 GENERAL TIP

If you feel this exercise more in your lower back than your upper back, you are probably using too much weight.

CHANGE IT UP

Inverted row–A great bodyweight alternative to the barbell row is an inverted row. Set up a barbell in a rack at about waist height. Hang underneath the bar so your body is in a straight line with your heels on the ground and your arms fully extended. Pull your chest toward the bar, pause at the top of the motion, and return to the starting position.

Underhand barbell row–For a different feel, use an underhand grip while barbell rowing. The exercise is performed the same way.

SEATED CABLE ROW

PRIMARY MUSCLES: LATISSIMUS DORSI, TERES MAJOR, AND RHOMBOIDS

The seated cable row is well-known among beginners and advanced lifters alike. It's an easy-to-use row variation that is available in most gyms and allows you to experiment with different grips. It's an excellent, versatile option for any bodybuilding program.

INSTRUCTIONS

1. Sit facing the seated cable row machine with your feet resting on the foot pad.
2. Grasp the handles with an overhand or neutral grip, depending on the handle.
3. Sit in an upright position with your torso perpendicular to the floor, knees slightly bent, and arms extended directly out in front of you. This is the starting position.
4. Begin the movement by pulling the handle toward your abdomen. Once the handle reaches your abdomen, return to the starting position.

Common Mistakes and How to Avoid Them

Mistake: Rounding your upper back

You want to maintain an upright position for the entire duration of the rep. Some people make the mistake of letting their backs round when returning to the starting position so they gain a longer range of motion. But in this case, you want to use only the range of motion that allows you to maintain a neutral spine.

To change the angle of the pull and muscle activation, place a box on the seat pad so you are elevated when you perform the exercise.

CHANGE IT UP

Wide-grip seated cable row– You may have various bars and grips at your disposal, and it's a good idea to try multiple grips throughout the year.

Single-arm seated cable row– The single-arm variation is an excellent exercise to do on an occasional basis.

NEUTRAL-GRIP LAT PULLDOWN

PRIMARY MUSCLES: LATISSIMUS DORSI (LATS)

The neutral grip, my favorite lat pulldown variation, activates different parts of the muscles. Plus it's a little easier on the shoulder joints. You can use wide and/or narrow neutral grips, depending on availability.

INSTRUCTIONS

1. Attach a neutral-grip handle (palms facing each other) to a lat pulldown tower.
2. Sit facing the machine with your legs positioned under the pads. Grip the overhead handle.
3. Arch your back slightly while pulling the handle down and toward your upper chest.
4. Once the bar touches your upper chest, slowly return to the starting position.

Common Mistakes and How to Avoid Them

Mistake: Pulling toward your stomach

People sometimes make the common mistake of pulling the handle down toward their stomach. To maximize lat activation, you want keep the chest high and pull toward the upper-chest/collarbone area.

 GENERAL TIP

Get a good stretch at the top of the movement between each rep.

Use multiple grips–Most gyms have multiple neutral-grip handles ranging from wide or narrow to angled or straight. Experiment with all of them and find which one feels the best.

Hammer Strength high row– If your gym has a Hammer Strength high row, you have the opportunity to exercise with a combination of a pulldown and row. It makes for a great alternative to the neutral-grip pulldown.

CHEST-SUPPORTED ROW

PRIMARY MUSCLES: LATISSIMUS DORSI (LATS), TERES MAJOR, AND RHOMBOIDS

The chest-supported row is one of the simplest and most effective exercises in the book. The exercise is easy on the shoulders and lower back, so everyone from your grandmother to a world-class bodybuilder can benefit from it.

INSTRUCTIONS

1. Sit erect with your feet flat on the floor and press your torso against the chest pad of the chest-supported row machine.

2. Extend your arms directly in front of you and grasp the handles with an overhand or neutral grip. This is the starting position.

3. Pull the handles back as far as possible toward your chest or abdomen. Return to the starting position.

Common Mistakes and How to Avoid Them

Mistake: Leaning back, away from the pad

The chest-supported row is one of the easiest exercises in the gym, but people sometimes lean away from the pad, which is a mistake. Keep your chest supported on the pad throughout the entire set. Sometimes placing your feet behind you (instead of in front) can help keep you upright.

 GENERAL TIP

Most chest-supported row machines have an adjustable seat. Make sure the seat is in a comfortable position for your height. A simple seat adjustment can make this exercise a lot more effective.

Inverted row–The inverted row can be a great bodyweight alternative to the chest-supported row. Perform an inverted row by setting up a barbell in a rack at about waist height. Position yourself hanging underneath the bar so your body is in a straight line with your heels on the ground and your arms fully extended. Pull your chest toward the bar, pause at the top of the motion, and return to the starting position.

T-bar row–If you want to go old school, you can slide a barbell into a corner and do T-bar rows. You can move a lot of weight this way; however, this exercise is a little more difficult to execute properly. To perform the T-bar row, position a bar into a corner to prevent it from moving and load weight on the opposite end. Stand over the bar and place a Double D cable attachment next to the collar. Take an athletic stance and pull the weight toward your upper abdomen.

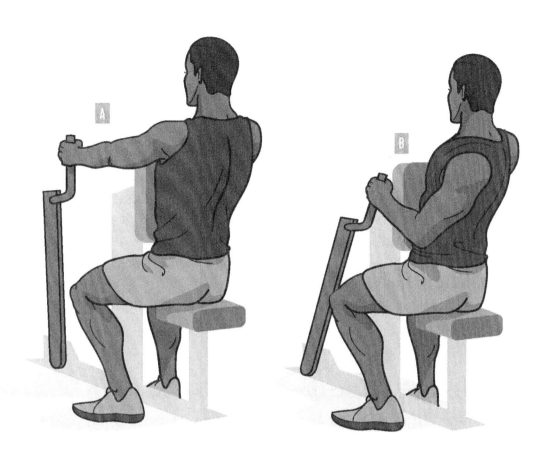

SINGLE-ARM LAT PULLDOWN

PRIMARY MUSCLES: LATISSIMUS DORSI (LATS)

The single-arm lat pulldown is one of the most underrated pulldown variations. Over the years, I have found this exercise to be great for people who don't feel their lats working during traditional lat pulldowns or pull-ups. The single-arm lat pulldown allows you to focus on each side individually, making it easier to engage the lats. This not only helps build balance between the left and right sides, but it also increases the difficulty of the exercise.

INSTRUCTIONS

1. Attach a single D-handle to a lat pulldown tower.
2. Sit facing the machine with your legs positioned under the pads. Grip the overhead handle.
3. Slightly arch your back while pulling the bar down and toward your upper chest.
4. Once the handle reaches your upper chest area, slowly return to the starting position.
5. Repeat with the other arm.

Common Mistakes and How to Avoid Them

Mistake: Turning too much toward the working side

Although it's a single-arm exercise, you want to keep your shoulders square and your torso vertical.

 GENERAL TIP

With this variation, it's easier to feel the muscle working. Strangely enough, sometimes if you touch the working lat with your free hand, it enhances the mind-muscle connection even more. This is a technique rarely discussed, but feeling the muscle work inside and out allows you to maintain tension where it belongs.

⤬ CHANGE IT UP

Single-arm underhand or neutral-grip pulldown–Using a D-handle allows you to pull down in any wrist position. You can pull with an underhand, overhand, or neutral grip.

One-arm pull-up–Admittedly, this is a very difficult exercise. However, if you can work up to being able to do a full set of one-arm pull-ups, you'll have accomplished an impressive feat of strength. I've never been able to do more than a couple of reps at a time.

BACK EXTENSION

PRIMARY MUSCLES: LOWER BACK

The back extension provides a great way to isolate the lower back in the safest way possible. You can do this exercise with your bodyweight or add weight by holding a dumbbell on your chest during the movement. A strong lower back helps prevent back pain.

INSTRUCTIONS

1. Lie facedown on a back extension bench. Place your ankles under the roller pads with your hips resting on the support pad. This is the starting position.

2. With your body straight, cross your arms in front of you and bend your torso forward toward the ground. Once you reach the point where you risk rounding your back, reverse the movement to return to the starting position.

Common Mistakes and How to Avoid Them

Mistake: Hyperextending at the top of the movement

Although the exercise is called a back extension, you want to avoid going into hyperextension at the top of the movement. You should extend only until your spine is in a neutral position. Continuing the extension does not add any extra training effect for the muscles and can put a lot of unnecessary strain on the lower back.

 GENERAL TIP

You can cross your arms in front of you on your chest, put them behind your head, or let them hang down by your sides.

Kettlebell swing–If you have access to a kettlebell, a great exercise to do in place of back extensions is kettlebell swings, which target your lower back, glutes, and hamstrings. Stand with your feet shoulder-width apart and knees slightly bent. Hold a kettlebell between your legs using a two-handed overhand grip. Maintain a slight arch in your lower back, and shift your hips back until the kettlebell is between and behind your legs. Squeeze your glutes, and drive your hips forward to swing the weight up to about shoulder height. Reverse the movement by letting the weight swing back between your legs as you slightly bend your knees and drive your hips back.

Reverse hyper–The reverse hyper is more commonly done by powerlifters, but try it if your gym has this machine. It's a great exercise to build the lower back and hamstrings. Place your feet in the straps and your chest on the top pad while grasping the handles. Your hips should hang off the back of the machine. Keep your legs straight and drive them up toward the ceiling by flexing the hips, glutes, and hamstrings. Reverse once your legs come up as high as they can.

LAT STRETCH

PRIMARY MUSCLES: BACK

When you focus on building muscle and strength in the lats, it can leave them tight and bunched up. This can cause poor overhead mobility, bad posture, and shoulder pain. The lat stretch is simple and easy to perform. I like to do this stretch after every upper-body workout.

INSTRUCTIONS

1. Stand facing a fixed bar or sturdy support.
2. Grab the bar or support at about waist height with two hands.
3. Allow your hips to fall back while you bend over. Lean your torso toward the bar/support. Hold the stretch.

Common Mistakes and How to Avoid Them

Mistake: Not being relaxed

Holding too much tension in the muscles during stretching, including the lat stretch, is never a good idea. Make sure you relax the lats and allow them to actually stretch.

 GENERAL TIP

Move your hips from side to side to enhance the stretch.

🔀 CHANGE IT UP

Foam roll lats–The lats are one of my favorite areas for soft-tissue work. Lie on your side with a foam roller tucked underneath your armpit. Apply pressure, and slowly roll from your armpit to your lower lats. Repeat on the other side. Spend more time on areas that need it.

ABS AND CORE

"How do I get six-pack abs?" is one of the questions people often ask me. Everyone has a six-pack whether they do traditional abs exercises or not. The trouble is, most people can't *see* their abs because of an excess layer of body fat.

Just because your abs are visible when you have low body fat does not mean you have a large amount of abdominal strength or muscular development. Your abs are just like every other muscle in the body; they need to be consistently challenged in training in order to grow and get stronger. Dieting may make your abs visible, but it is a consistent overload that makes them really stand out!

The benefits of a strong core go beyond just looks. The core is the central link connecting the upper and lower body. Whether you lift something off the ground, twist, punch, kick, or swing a golf club, it all requires core strength. In addition, having a strong core is one of the best ways to prevent lower-back pain.

Since the core is activated during other exercises, it eliminates the need to add a specific warm-up or cool down.

FOREARM PLANK

PRIMARY MUSCLES: ABDOMINALS

The plank is an isometric exercise, which means it doesn't require any movement. However, don't let the simplicity of this exercise confuse you; it's a very effective way to improve core stability and prevent lower-back pain. Since it doesn't require any movement or equipment, it's also one of the safest and easiest core exercises when done correctly.

INSTRUCTIONS

1. Lie facedown on the floor, then lift yourself up using your toes and forearms. Your arms should be bent at 90 degrees with your elbows directly under your shoulders and your wrists aligned with your elbows.

2. Once in position, brace your core hard like you are preparing to get punched in the stomach. Flex your glutes and thigh muscles while continuing to breathe normally.

3. Keep your body straight at all times, and hold this position for the duration of the set.

Common Mistakes and How to Avoid Them

Mistake: Allowing your hips to sag

When executing the plank, it's essential to keep your body in a straight line at all times. Don't allow your hips to raise or lower due to fatigue.

 GENERAL TIP

It's common when creating full-body tension to forget to breathe. Remember to breathe normally. Focusing on breathing at regular intervals also helps you stay relaxed by taking your mind off how long you need to hold each rep and any discomfort.

⤨ CHANGE IT UP

Push-up position plank–This alternative plank position will incorporate some chest and shoulder stability in addition to the core work. To perform the Push-up position plank, assume a push-up position (body supported by your hands and toes while maintaining a straight back) and hold.

Feet-elevated one-leg plank– To make the plank more difficult, raise your feet up on a box. Or to take things to the next level, elevate only one leg at a time to increase the difficulty.

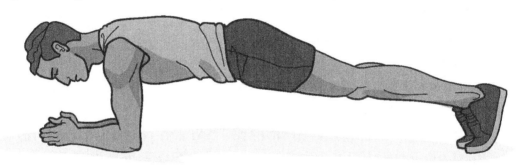

DECLINE SIT-UP

PRIMARY MUSCLES: ABDOMINALS

The decline sit-up is one of my favorite abs exercises. It allows you to use gravity to make the standard sit-up more difficult and effective. When training abs, it's not enough to perform easy exercises with extremely high reps. Like any other muscles, the abdominals need to experience periods of high resistance to grow and gain strength.

INSTRUCTIONS

1. Secure your legs at the end of the decline bench and lie down. Cross your arms on your chest. This is the starting position.

2. Push your lower back down on the bench to better isolate your abdominal muscles. Begin to roll your shoulders off the bench.

3. Continue to sit up until your arms come in contact with your knees. Hold the top position for one second.

4. Roll down slowly to the starting position.

Common Mistakes and How to Avoid Them

Mistake: Not focusing on the way down

To get the most out of this exercise, return to the starting position in a controlled fashion and avoid using momentum. Your core should remain tight throughout the entire rep.

 GENERAL TIP

The higher the incline, the more difficult the exercise and vice versa. Start with a small incline and slowly increase the incline as you get stronger.

Sit-up—If decline sit-ups are a little too challenging right now, you can do regular sit-ups. Once you get to the point where regular sit-ups become easy, jump over to the decline sit-up.

Weighted decline sit-up—To make the decline sit-up more difficult, you can add weight to this exercise by holding a plate on your chest or behind your head. I warn you, there are not many exercises more challenging. If you get to that point, your core will be as hard as granite!

BACK-SUPPORTED KNEE RAISE

PRIMARY MUSCLES: ABDOMINALS

The back-supported knee raise is one of the best overall abs exercises. The movement specifically targets the lower section of the abdominals, and it also incorporates some hip flexor muscles. Back support provides protection to the lower back and helps you maintain the correct form.

INSTRUCTIONS

1. Support your body by resting your elbows on the pads of the vertical knee raise machine. Position your back against the back support.

2. Raise your knees to your chest, rounding your lower back in order to contract your abdominal core. The key is to get your knees as high as possible.

3. Once your knees come up to your chest (or as high as possible), lower them with control. Make sure your feet extend all the way between reps.

Common Mistakes and How to Avoid Them

Mistake: Using too much momentum

The key to this exercise is using a slow and controlled motion and not swinging the legs up and down. Make sure your abs are contracting and causing your legs to move. With this exercise, it's important not to just go from point A to point B. You want to feel the muscles working.

 GENERAL TIP

You can do this exercise by raising your knees—or for increased difficulty, your outstretched legs.

Hanging knee raise–As a variation, try this exercise hanging from a pull-up bar. All the other instructions are the same, except there is no back support. Hanging from a pull-up bar also incorporates some grip and forearm training.

Hanging toes to bar–This is the granddaddy of all leg-raise exercises. For the most difficult version of this exercise, hang from a pull-up bar and try to raise your legs so high that your toes touch the bar. No wonder it's popular in CrossFit competitions. To build your abs, you want to maintain correct form and limit your use of momentum.

ROPE CABLE CRUNCH

PRIMARY MUSCLES: ABDOMINALS

When I think of rope cable crunches, the image of Arnold Schwarzenegger doing tons of reps in the movie *Pumping Iron* comes to mind. Rope cable crunches, a classical abdominals builder, can be a little tricky to master at first. The key is to avoid rocking the torso up and down. You may not feel the crunches working right away, but once you get the hang of them, rope cable crunches will be a game changer for your abs workouts!

INSTRUCTIONS

1. Kneel below a high pulley with a rope attachment.
2. Grasp both ends of the rope. Pull it down so that your hands holding the rope are by your face.
3. Flex your hips slightly and allow the weight to stretch out your lower back. This will be your starting position.
4. With your hips fixed, bend your waist as you contract the abs in a crunch motion. Your elbows should move toward the middle of your thighs. Make sure that you maintain constant abdominal tension. Hold the contraction for one second.
5. Slowly return to the starting position.

Common Mistakes and How to Avoid Them

Mistake: Using too much weight

Using too much weight means you will lift the weight with other muscles instead of focusing on your abs.

GENERAL TIP

You can do this exercise kneeling or standing. Find the method that works best for you.

CHANGE IT UP

Machine crunch–Machine crunches are a great alternative to the rope cable crunch. Sit on the machine, placing your feet under the pads, and grab the top handles. Crunch your upper torso toward your legs, and contract your abdominals. Make sure you use your abs to move the weight, not your arms.

Basic crunch–This method remains an effective abs exercise. Plus you can do it anywhere.

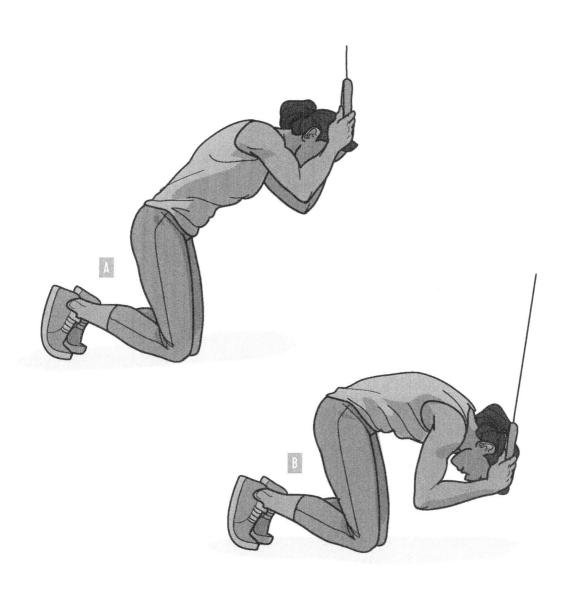

AB WHEEL

PRIMARY MUSCLES: ABDOMINALS

The ab wheel, which is underused yet brutally effective, is my favorite abs exercise. If your gym doesn't have one, you can buy an inexpensive one online. It's worth the investment to have one in your gym bag. You can also use a barbell with 10-pound plates on each side.

INSTRUCTIONS

1. Place the ab roller on the floor in front of you and kneel with your knees about hip-width apart. Grasp the ab roller with both hands. This is your starting position.

2. Slowly roll the ab roller in front of you, stretching your body into a straight position. Like with a plank, make sure the movement isn't coming from your spine or from your hips. Maintain a neutral spine throughout the set.

3. Go down as low as you can without any part of your body (except your knees and feet) touching the floor.

4. Pause at the end of the roll-out and pull yourself back to the starting position using your core. Keep your abs tight at all times.

Common Mistakes and How to Avoid Them

Mistake: Hips sagging

This is a tough exercise when done correctly, and the biggest mistake is allowing your hips to sag. Keep your core tight and your glutes flexed to help keep your torso in a straight line.

GENERAL TIP

If rolling out to a full extension is too hard at first, you can start by going only halfway. Slowly work your way to completing the full range of motion.

CHANGE IT UP

Plank–A traditional plank works well as a bodyweight alternative for the ab wheel.

Ab wheel with feet–If you get really strong using your knees, you can try this exercise standing and using your feet. All the same directions apply.

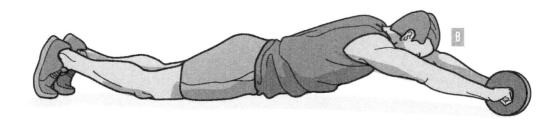

BICYCLE CRUNCH

PRIMARY MUSCLES: ABDOMINALS (OBLIQUES)

Bicycle crunches are one of the most common abdominal exercises, and I understand why. Although the movement is known for its amazing impact on the obliques, bicycle crunches target your entire core. Speed is the enemy here. Make sure you go slowly and focus on proper technique.

INSTRUCTIONS

1. Lie flat on the floor with your lower back pressed to the ground. Put your hands behind your head with your elbows flared out to the sides. Your knees should be bent at 90 degrees with your feet flat off the floor. This is your starting position.

2. Lift your shoulders into the crunch position while simultaneously using a bicycle pedal motion to kick forward with the right leg and retract the left knee. Bring your right elbow close to your left knee by crunching to the side.

3. Go back to the initial starting position.

4. Crunch to the opposite side as you cycle your legs and this time lift your left elbow to your right knee.

5. Continue alternating in this manner until you've completed the recommended reps for each side.

Common Mistakes and How to Avoid Them

Mistake: Hip rotation

People tend to rotate their hips on each rep, but your torso should do all of the rotation. Remember to drive your legs straight out while keeping your lower back pressed into the floor for the entire set.

 GENERAL TIP

If you feel a strain in your neck while doing this exercise, chances are you're pulling on it with your hands. Try doing the exercise with your fingers placed gently behind your ears.

CHANGE IT UP

Dumbbell side bend–This involves holding a dumbbell in one hand and bending down toward that side. Allow the dumbbell to reach about knee level before using the opposite oblique to raise it back up. Keep the arm holding the dumbbell straight for the duration of the rep.

HOLLOW-BODY HOLD

PRIMARY MUSCLES: ABDOMINALS

Gymnasts have long used this abdominal exercise to strengthen their core. In fact, the hollow-body hold is one of the first exercises they learn. It's a foundational position that involves bracing your abs and creating total-body tension, strengthening the entire abdominal region without compromising the lower back. This is one exercise that is a lot harder than it looks!

INSTRUCTIONS

1. Lie on your back with your arms and legs extended.
2. Contract your abs, pulling your belly button toward the floor. Your arms and legs should be held straight out and your hands and toes pointed.
3. Slowly raise your legs and shoulders from the ground, followed by your arms and head. Your lower back must remain in contact with the floor.
4. Hold the position with your shoulders and legs raised off the ground for the duration of the set, and return to the floor.

Common Mistakes and How to Avoid Them

Mistake: Allowing space under your lower back

This can be a tricky exercise. The biggest key to doing it properly is to push your lower back flat against the ground at all times while doing this exercise.

 GENERAL TIP

Begin with your arms and legs held 1 to 2 feet from the floor and slowly develop strength until they can be held lower without compromising your form.

Lying leg-lift hold–Instead of the hollow-body hold, try the timed leg-lift holds that you used to do in gym class. Lie flat on the ground on your back with your legs extended. Keeping your legs straight, lift them about 4 to 6 inches off the ground. Hold that position for the desired amount of time, then return your feet to the floor.

CABLE PALLOF PRESS

PRIMARY MUSCLES: ABDOMINALS (OBLIQUES)

The cable Pallof press is probably the most deceptive exercise in this book. It doesn't look very difficult, and you may even wonder why it's included at all. Prepare to be humbled. This exercise is all about anti-rotation and strengthening your obliques.

INSTRUCTIONS

1. Position a D-handle attachment to a cable pulley machine at about shoulder height.
2. Stand perpendicular to the cable machine and grab the handle with both hands. The handle should be in front of your body, with the resistance pulling to the side.
3. Step away from the tower so that you are about an arm's length away from the pulley, keeping the weight's tension on the cable.
4. With your feet hip-width apart and knees slightly bent, pull the cable to the middle of your chest. This will be your starting position.
5. Push the cable away from your chest, fully extending both arms. Your core should be tight and engaged.
6. Hold the rep for several seconds. Return to the starting position.
7. After a completed set, turn in the opposite direction and repeat the exercise for the other side.

Common Mistakes and How to Avoid Them

Mistake: Allowing your hips and torso to rotate toward the weight

The Pallof press is an anti-rotation exercise based on maintaining a neutral spine and keeping your hips square and still. As soon as you move your hips or twist your torso, the exercise loses its effectiveness.

 GENERAL TIP

Brace your core to reinforce full body tension. You should be so tight that if someone ran into you, you would hardly budge.

 CHANGE IT UP

Band Pallof press—Try doing the Pallof press with a band instead of a cable attachment.

Kneeling cable Pallof press—To add an extra layer of difficulty, perform the press from a kneeling or half-kneeling position.

LYING LEG LIFT

PRIMARY MUSCLES: ABDOMINALS

I have a love/hate relationship with lying leg lifts. They bring back memories of doing hundreds of reps during wrestling practice in high school, but I love that they are a great core exercise that doesn't require any equipment. You can do them anywhere and anytime, which takes away any excuse to not get them done!

INSTRUCTIONS

1. Lie on your back, flat on the ground with your legs extended in front of you.
2. Place your hands on the floor by your hips. This will be the starting position.
3. Keep your legs outstretched as straight as possible with your knees slightly bent but locked.
4. Raise your legs to a 90-degree angle with the floor and hold the contraction for one second.
5. Slowly lower your legs to the starting position. Control is everything; don't rush.

Common Mistakes and How to Avoid Them

Mistake: Arching your back

Like the Hollow-Body Hold, keep your lower back flat on the ground for the duration of the rep. If you start to arch your back, you'll remove some of the tension from the abs.

 GENERAL TIP

At the top of the rep, raise your hips toward the ceiling to increase the difficulty.

CHANGE IT UP

Bench lying leg lifts—Try leg lifts on a bench instead of the floor. All the same directions apply.

SIDE PLANK

PRIMARY MUSCLES: ABDOMINALS (OBLIQUES)

There are very few exercises as good for your core as the side plank, which is often overlooked in favor of the traditional plank. In my opinion, it's a good idea to incorporate both variations into your program. Like the traditional plank, the side plank is an isometric exercise that helps improve core stability, and it has the unique advantage of also targeting the obliques. Because the side plank requires you to work one side of the body at a time, it's a great way to detect a muscular imbalance.

INSTRUCTIONS

1. Lie on one side with your legs stacked one on top of the other and your body straight.

2. Lift your body using your forearm and elbow to maintain stability.

3. Keep your body straight and hold this position for the duration of the set.

4. Repeat on the other side.

Common Mistakes and How to Avoid Them

Mistake: Allowing your hips to sag

With all plank variations, the biggest mistake is allowing the hips to drop. Maintain core tightness and keep your body in a straight line.

 GENERAL TIP

Use a yoga mat to make the exercise more comfortable on your forearms/elbows.

Elevated side plank– Elevate your feet on a box, bench, or chair to make this exercise more challenging.

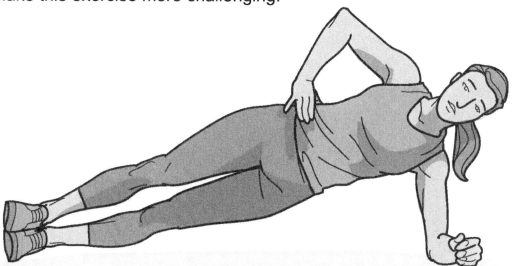

ARMS AND SHOULDERS

Band Dislocation

Overhead Barbell Press

Seated Dumbbell Shoulder Press

Dumbbell Side Raise

Rope Face Pull

Cable Side Raise

Dumbbell Shrug

Dumbbell Hammer Curl

EZ Bar Curl

Cable Triceps Pressdown

Lying EZ Bar Triceps Extension

EZ Bar Preacher Curl

Dead Hang

Building muscular arms and shoulders is what bodybuilding is all about. Arms and shoulders are the epitome of "show muscles" and the primary goal of most bodybuilders. Nothing looks more impressive in a T-shirt. Unfortunately, most beginners train these muscles with so many exercises and with such frequency that it becomes counterproductive. What they don't understand is that the arms and shoulders are made up of relatively small muscles that respond best to being trained in moderation.

The upper arm is made up of two muscle groups: the biceps and triceps. Although the biceps get all the attention, it's the triceps that make up the bulk of arm mass. In other words, if you want big arms, it's important to focus on building big triceps. Meanwhile, the shoulders are made up of three muscles called the anterior deltoid, middle deltoid, and posterior deltoid. Each has unique functions that require a wide range of exercises for maximum shoulder development.

BAND DISLOCATION

PRIMARY MUSCLES: SHOULDERS

The shoulder is one of the most mobile and most frequently injured joints in the human body. This is especially true for those of us who lift heavy weights. To help avoid injury, it's important to make sure your shoulders are not stiff heading into an upper-body workout. Band dislocation is a great exercise to loosen and get them moving through an active range of motion. It's a good idea to do them every day.

INSTRUCTIONS

1. Hold the ends of a light resistance band in each hand. Begin with the band in front of your torso with your hands down at your sides.

2. Stretch the band slightly to increase the tension. Your hands should be wider than shoulder-width apart.

3. While keeping your shoulders retracted and arms straight, begin to raise the band overhead and back down behind you.

4. Once you come to the end of the range of motion, return to the starting position.

Common Mistakes and How to Avoid Them

Mistake: Not keeping constant tension on the band

It's important to keep constant tension on the band, avoiding any slack throughout the exercise.

 GENERAL TIP

As you improve, you can grab the band with a narrower grip to increase tension.

 CHANGE IT UP

Broomstick or PVC pipe dislocation–I personally like using a resistance band, but you can also do this movement with a simple broomstick or a long PVC pipe.

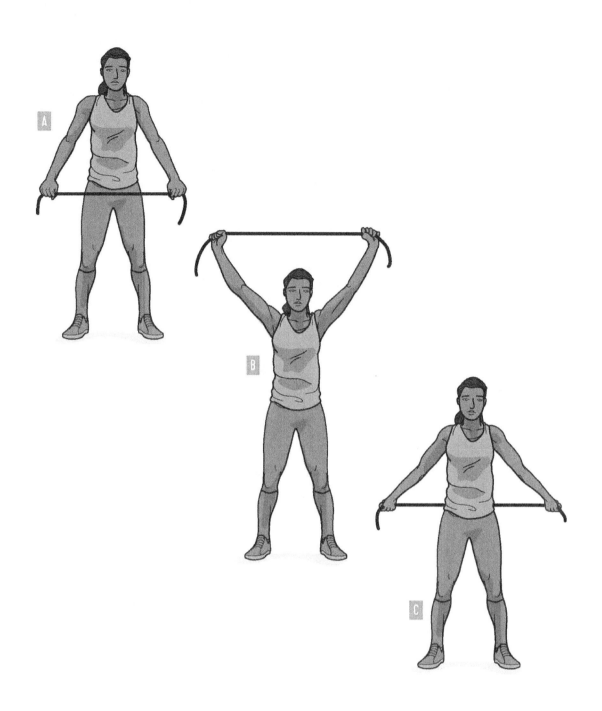

OVERHEAD BARBELL PRESS

PRIMARY MUSCLES: SHOULDERS

The overhead barbell press is the king of shoulder exercises. Nothing will put meat across your entire shoulder area like the overhead press. This is one of the few shoulder exercises that can be overloaded with heavy weights, but it is also an exercise that can cause shoulder injuries if form is not on point. Make sure you warm up well and have good technique before adding weight to the bar.

INSTRUCTIONS

1. Start with a barbell in a rack at about chest level. Grasp the barbell with an overhand grip, slightly wider than shoulder width, and position it in front of your neck at the collarbone. This is the starting position.

2. Take a deep breath, brace your core, flex your glutes, and press the bar up until your arms are extended overhead. At that point, bring your head and chest through the bar.

3. Return the bar to the starting position.

Common Mistakes and How to Avoid Them

Mistake: Using your legs to drive the bar

Some people inadvertently turn the overhead barbell press into what is called a "push press." A push press uses the legs to lift the barbell overhead, which takes some of the tension off the shoulders. In this exercise, though, you want your shoulders to do the lifting. To avoid relying on your legs, maintain a slight knee bend and limit any lower-body movement.

 GENERAL TIP

Find a foot position that is comfortable. I personally like a narrow stance, slightly less than shoulder width, but that is not required.

CHANGE IT UP

Machine shoulder press–If your gym has a machine shoulder press, it can be a nice variation to throw in from time to time. Sit on the shoulder press machine and grab the handles. Press the handles overhead as you extend your arms. Once you reach full arm extension, return the handles to the starting position.

Seated barbell shoulder press– You can do this exercise another way if your gym has a seated shoulder press bench. Have a spotter assist you by taking the barbell out of the rack.

SEATED DUMBBELL SHOULDER PRESS

PRIMARY MUSCLES: SHOULDERS

The seated dumbbell shoulder press is a great exercise to build muscle and strength across each shoulder. It allows for each side to work individually, which may reveal muscle imbalances or stability issues. The exercise also causes less stress on the lower back because the movement is from a seated position.

INSTRUCTIONS

1. Sit on a bench with a back support.
2. Hold two dumbbells at shoulder level with an overhand grip and your palms facing forward. This is the starting position.
3. Press the dumbbells overhead.
4. Once your arms are straight and fully extended, hold for a second, then return to the starting position.

Common Mistakes and How to Avoid Them

Mistake: Leaning back too far

It's okay to have a slight arch in your lower back during the movement, but your torso should remain vertical to properly target the shoulder muscles. If you lean back too far, some of the focus is shifted to the upper chest and also puts the lower back at risk of injury. If you feel like you need to lean back in order to lift the weight, chances are the weight is too heavy.

 GENERAL TIP

To save some of your energy for the exercise, ask someone to help you get the dumbbells into the starting position.

🔀 CHANGE IT UP

Standing dumbbell shoulder press–Try this exercise standing, and use a spotter's help to get the dumbbells into position.

One-arm dumbbell shoulder press– For a harder variation, you can use one dumbbell at a time. The movement is performed the same way.

DUMBBELL SIDE RAISE

PRIMARY MUSCLES: SHOULDERS (LATERAL DELTS)

This may surprise you, but the dumbbell side raise is one of the most important exercises for a bodybuilder. Building the medial deltoids helps create the "capped" shoulder look desired by so many bodybuilders, and the dumbbell side raise is the best way to accomplish it. It's as close to a must-do as any other isolation exercise in this book.

INSTRUCTIONS

1. Stand with a straight back and your rib cage down, holding one dumbbell in each hand. (To bring your rib cage down, brace your core like you're getting ready for a punch.) This is the starting position.

2. Leading with the elbows slightly bent, raise the dumbbells to the side until your arms are parallel to the ground.

3. Pause for one second before returning to the starting position.

Common Mistakes and How to Avoid Them

Mistake: Shrugging your shoulders during the movement

Try not to shrug your shoulders as you lift your arms. Shrugging takes some of the tension away from the side delts and into the trapezius (the muscle between your neck and shoulders). Keep your shoulders retracted and locked down. The goal is to keep all of the movement in your arms.

 GENERAL TIP

On the way up, tilt the dumbbell so that your pinky comes up first. Your hand should look like you are pouring a cup of water.

⤫ CHANGE IT UP

Band side raise–Use a resistance band for banded side raises. Start by standing on one end of the resistance band. Hold the other end in your hand on the same side, and follow the instructions for the dumbbell side raise.

Seated dumbbell side raise–One of my favorite ways to do dumbbell side raises is from a seated position on the edge of a bench. The execution is the same.

ROPE FACE PULL

PRIMARY MUSCLES: SHOULDERS (REAR DELTS)

The rope face pull is a great exercise to target the rear delts, keep the shoulders healthy, and improve posture. When you do a lot of pressing exercises for the chest and shoulders, it's important to balance them with an equal or greater amount of pulling.

INSTRUCTIONS

1. Start with a rope attachment, connected to a high cable, at about face level.

2. Grasp both ends of the rope attachment with an overhand grip. Step back so that your arms are fully extended. This is the starting position.

3. Pull the rope toward your face, keeping your elbows high.

4. Once you pull back as far as you can, spread the rope and hold it for one second before returning to the starting position.

Common Mistakes and How to Avoid Them

Mistake 1: Pulling too low

It's a common mistake to pull the rope toward the chest. To properly target the rear delts, keep your elbows high and pull toward your face.

Mistake 2: Going too heavy

The face pull is not a power exercise. Use a weight you can control through the full range of motion. Going too heavy forces you to use your lower back to lift the weight, which defeats the purpose of the exercise.

On the last rep, pause at the end of the motion when the rope is near your face and hold it for 10 seconds before slowly returning to the starting position.

Band pull-apart–Use straight arms to pull a resistance band to your sides horizontally until it reaches your chest.

CABLE SIDE RAISE

PRIMARY MUSCLES: SHOULDERS (LATERAL DELTS)

Like the Dumbbell Side Raise, the cable variation is an excellent exercise to target the lateral head of the delts. One of the major benefits to using cables is that they provide constant muscle tension. But unlike the dumbbell side raise, which gets progressively harder the higher the hand is raised, the cable variation offers maximum tension right from the start.

INSTRUCTIONS

1. Stand with a straight back using one hand to hold a cable attachment in front of you at waist level. This is the starting position.

2. Raise that arm, keeping your elbow slightly bent until it is parallel to the floor. It's important to maintain the arm angle during the movement.

3. Pause for one second, then return to the starting position. Repeat on the other side.

Common Mistakes and How to Avoid Them

Mistake: Going too fast

Since the cable provides constant tension, there is a tendency to speed through the reps. Use a slow and controlled tempo to get the most out of this exercise.

 GENERAL TIP

With the nonworking arm, hold on to the machine for support, and lean toward the working side. Remember to keep a straight back.

 CHANGE IT UP

Machine side raise—Using a side raise machine is an excellent variation. Sit on the machine with your forearms and elbows pressed against the pads. Move your upper arms out to either side, away from your body. When your upper arms are parallel to the floor, return to the starting position.

DUMBBELL SHRUG

PRIMARY MUSCLES: TRAPEZIUS

There are few exercises as simple to perform as the dumbbell shrug. Not only that but shrugs are great for building the upper part of the trapezius muscle (the muscle between your neck and shoulders). Big, developed traps go a long way toward balancing out a bodybuilding (or muscular) physique.

INSTRUCTIONS

1. Stand erect with a dumbbell in each hand, palms facing your torso and arms extended alongside your body. This is the starting position.

2. Lift the dumbbells by elevating your shoulders as high as possible. Try to bring your shoulders up to your ears. Hold this position for a second before returning to the starting position.

Common Mistakes and How to Avoid Them

Mistake: Rolling your shoulders

Rolling your shoulders is a dangerous and less effective way to perform the movement. As the name suggests, just shrug your shoulders up and down in a straight line.

 GENERAL TIP

If grip strength is your limiting factor, you can use straps to take the grip out of the movement. Another option to help with grip is to apply some lifting chalk to your hands. This way, you get the added benefit of training your grip strength as well.

Barbell shrug–A barbell variation allows you to load the most weight. Trap bar shrug–The trap bar, a diamond- or hexagonal-shaped weight lifting tool, is an option that puts your hands in a more comfortable position at your side.

DUMBBELL HAMMER CURL

PRIMARY MUSCLES: BICEPS

The dumbbell hammer curl is one of the best all-around biceps exercises. What is unique about the hammer curl is the neutral grip. This incorporates the brachialis, which is a muscle between the biceps and triceps that flexes the elbow joint. Training your brachialis is a great way to make your arms appear bigger because the brachialis actually pushes apart your biceps and triceps as it develops. The hammer curl also incorporates some forearm work.

INSTRUCTIONS

1. Stand erect, holding two dumbbells using a closed, neutral grip (palms facing body). Position the dumbbells along your thighs with your arms fully extended. This is the starting position.

2. Keeping the dumbbells in a neutral grip, curl them toward your shoulders. Pay attention to your elbows' position. Your elbows should remain steady at your side throughout the entire rep. Avoid letting them drift forward during the movement.

3. Once executed, lower the weights until your elbows are fully extended.

Common Mistakes and How to Avoid Them

Mistake: Elbows moving

If the weight is too heavy, the elbows tend to drift forward or out to the side during the rep. This shifts tension from the biceps to the shoulders. Be sure lock your elbows in place for the duration of the set.

 GENERAL TIP

To focus more on each arm, perform the exercise with one arm at a time.

CHANGE IT UP

Reverse curl–For this option, hold the barbell with a reverse or pronated grip (see here) to incorporate more forearm action than with a traditional curl.

EZ BAR CURL

PRIMARY MUSCLES: BICEPS

When many people think of curls, the EZ curl bar likely comes to mind. The advantage of the EZ bar variation is that it puts your wrists in a safe position, unlike regular barbell curls which force the wrists into an unnatural position and can cause pain. The angled grip of the EZ curl bar is perfect for overloading the biceps in a safe and effective way.

INSTRUCTIONS

1. Stand erect, grasping an EZ curl bar with a closed, underhand grip. The grip should be shoulder width so your arms touch the sides of your torso. Allow your arms to be fully extended. This is the starting position.

2. Curl the weight until the bar is near the front of your shoulders. Be mindful of your elbows' position. Don't let your elbows drift forward during the movement.

3. Once the bar reaches your shoulders, slowly lower it back to the starting position.

Common Mistakes and How to Avoid Them

Mistake: Rocking back and forth

You don't want your lower body to be part of the exercise. Only your arms should move while you curl the weight. Lock your legs and torso in place and prevent any rocking back and forth or arching in the lower back.

 GENERAL TIP

The EZ curl bar allows for multiple grips ranging from narrow to wide. Use different grips throughout the year.

⤨ CHANGE IT UP

Chin-ups–Underhand-grip pull-ups (chin-ups) are a great bodyweight variation.

Barbell curls–Try a traditional straight barbell if an EZ curl bar is not available.

CABLE TRICEPS PRESSDOWN

PRIMARY MUSCLES: TRICEPS

Although biceps get all the love, big triceps, major muscles in the upper arm, are essential if you want big arms. And when it comes to training the triceps, nothing is as simple or effective as the cable triceps pressdown. The good news is that, unlike many other triceps exercises, this one is easy on the joints.

INSTRUCTIONS

1. Attach a straight bar to a high pulley. Grab the bar at shoulder height using an overhand grip (palms facing down).

2. Stand with a straight torso and lean slightly forward. Place your upper arms close to your body and perpendicular to the ground. Your forearms, which are holding the bar, should point up toward the pulley. This is your starting position.

3. Press the bar down until your arms are fully extended. Your upper arms should always remain stationary next to your torso; only your forearms should move.

4. After pausing for one second at the bottom position, bring the bar slowly up to the starting position.

Common Mistakes and How to Avoid Them

Mistake: Allowing your elbows to come forward

The most common mistake with the triceps pressdown is allowing the elbows to drift forward. This shifts the focus from the triceps to the lats. Remember to lock your upper arms against your torso for the duration of the exercise.

Feel free to use a rope attachment or different grips (wide, narrow, underhand, etc.) when performing the triceps pressdown.

CHANGE IT UP

Bench dips—To try this alternative exercise, stand with your back perpendicular to a bench. Reach behind you and place both hands on the bench edge shoulder-width apart. Extend your legs in front of you while your arms support your upper body. (To increase the difficulty, elevate your feet by placing them on a box or bench.) Slowly lower your body by flexing the elbows until they reach a 90-degree angle. Using your triceps, lift yourself back to the starting position.

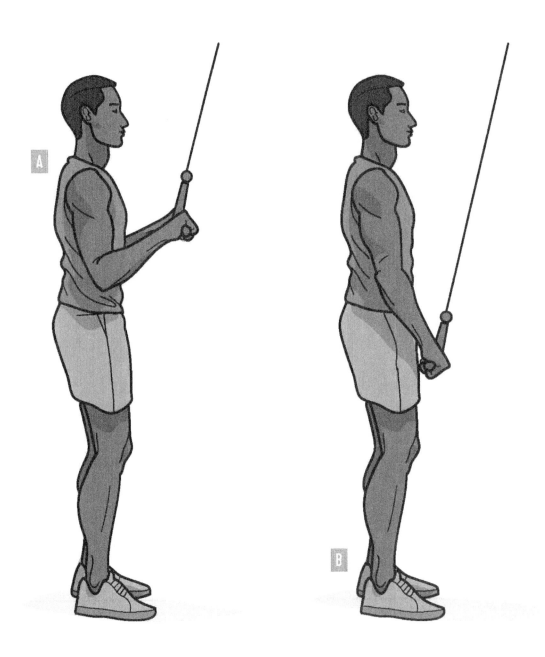

LYING EZ BAR TRICEPS EXTENSION

PRIMARY MUSCLES: TRICEPS

The lying EZ bar triceps extension, otherwise known as "the skullcrusher," is one of the best mass-building triceps exercises around. This is the exercise for when you want to put size on the back of your arms. The key is finding the right grip width and the range of motion that feels best. Some people experience elbow pain if this exercise is done incorrectly, so pay special attention to technique. SAFETY NOTE: Any time we are putting weight over our head, it's a good idea to have a spotter.

INSTRUCTIONS

1. Lie on your back on a horizontal bench and grasp an EZ curl bar with a closed, overhand grip at about shoulder width.

2. Position the bar over your chest with arms fully extended and locked. Your elbows should be pointed toward your knees. This is the starting position.

3. Keep your upper arms stationary as your elbows bend, bringing the bar toward your forehead.

4. Keep your wrists stiff and upper arms perpendicular to the floor for the duration of the rep.

5. Lower the bar until it almost touches your forehead, then return to the starting position using your triceps.

Common Mistakes and How to Avoid Them

Mistake: Too much elbow flare

With this exercise, you want to avoid allowing your elbows to flare out toward the sides. This turns it into a press, which incorporates more chest and less triceps.

 GENERAL TIP

You can lower the bar to your face, forehead, or even behind your head. All of the positions work. Find the position that feels best for you and use that.

CHANGE IT UP

Close-grip push-up–This is a great bodyweight variation and is executed the same way as a traditional push-up. The only difference is that you place your hands closer than shoulder-width apart to create the close grip.

Incline lying EZ bar triceps extension–If doing this exercise on a flbar at bench triceps causes elbow extensions pain, try it on a slight incline.

EZ BAR PREACHER CURL

PRIMARY MUSCLES: BICEPS

The preacher curl was made famous by Larry Scott, the first bodybuilder to win the Mr. Olympia international bodybuilding competition. It provides a unique angle to work the biceps and does so in a way that almost makes it impossible to cheat (unlike with regular curls). You may not be able to lift as much weight on a preacher curl, but it focuses on the biceps better than any other exercise.

INSTRUCTIONS

1. Start by standing or sitting on the stool connected to a preacher bench. Rest your arms on the support.

2. Position yourself so the armrest fits snugly under your armpits. Grasp the bar with an underhand grip and remove the barbell from the supports. This is the starting position.

3. Curl the bar toward your body.

4. Once the bar gets a couple of inches away from your shoulders, slowly lower it back to the starting position.

Common Mistakes and How to Avoid Them

Mistake: Not going all the way down

The unique angle of the preacher bench makes this exercise increasingly difficult at the bottom of the rep. Because of this, people tend to shortchange the movement and stop the rep about halfway down. Make sure you lower the weight all the way down until your arms are fully extended.

 GENERAL TIP

If you find yourself wanting to arch your back and lean away from the pad, don't sit in the connected seat. Instead, stand on your feet while keeping your chest pressed against the pad.

CHANGE IT UP

Dumbbell preacher curl—Try this alternative using dumbbells, following the same instructions.

DEAD HANG

PRIMARY MUSCLES: SHOULDERS AND FOREARMS

The dead hang is the simplest thing you can do to improve your shoulder health, overhead positioning, and grip strength while decompressing the spine at the same time. When you hang, gravity pulls the body down and away from the bar, which can help open up the shoulders and increase range of motion over time. The limiting factor initially will be grip strength, but that will catch up as a secondary benefit to improving your shoulder health.

INSTRUCTIONS

1. Grip an overhead bar with an overhand grip and your hands about shoulder-width apart. Relax the whole body, specifically reducing tension in your shoulders and lower back.

2. Keep your arms straight. Just relax and hang.

Common Mistakes and How to Avoid Them

Mistake: Not relaxing your shoulders

To get the greatest benefit from the exercise, allow the shoulders to relax and let go of any tension in the lats. I like to imagine that I'm lengthening my body as much as possible.

 GENERAL TIP

This is such a beneficial exercise for shoulder health that I recommend getting a doorway pull-up bar for your house and doing a dead hang every morning.

🔀 CHANGE IT UP

Lat pulldown stretch–If you can't hold your own weight in a dead hang position, you can do the same movement with a lat pulldown machine. With the machine version, you won't have gravity working in your favor, but you can adjust the weight to a manageable amount. All of the same directions apply. Just relax your shoulders and get a good stretch.

CHEST

Push-up
Barbell Bench Press
Dumbbell Flat & Incline Bench Press
Close-Grip Bench Press
Dumbbell Pullover
Parallel Bar Dip
Cable Crossover Fly
Machine Chest Press
Doorway Chest Stretch

People typically don't ask how much you can squat, curl, or row, but they will ask how much you can bench. It's all about chest training. Besides the biceps, no other muscle group receives as much attention. Let's face it, the barbell bench press is one of the most popular barbell exercises you can do.

In terms of chest growth, it's important to keep in mind that the pectorals are a muscle group with multiple attachment points requiring a variety of angles and exercises for maximum development. Simple adjustments such as bench angle can affect the muscle area that is most stimulated. For example, an incline bench press shifts more focus toward the upper chest than a flat bench press. (In my 12-week program, you'll use a mix of barbells, dumbbells, cables, machines, and bodyweight exercises to maximize muscle development.)

Having a strong and muscular chest has upsides beyond the gym or bodybuilding circuit, too. Chest strength comes into play anytime you push a heavy object, swim, swing a tennis racket, or even push yourself up off the ground. It makes day-to-day activities easier.

PUSH-UP

PRIMARY MUSCLES: CHEST

The push-up is an underrated exercise that can be a valuable tool in any training program. When you lower yourself with your hands and feet fixed to the ground, your scapula is free to move. This movement, combined with the required core stabilization, makes the push-up a perfect warm-up exercise.

INSTRUCTIONS

1. Lie on the floor facedown and place your hands on either side of your shoulders. Fully extend your arms to lift your torso.

2. Next, lower yourself until your chest almost touches the floor, making sure to keep your core tight.

3. Push up your arms again, lifting your upper body to the starting position.

Common Mistakes and How to Avoid Them

Mistake: Keep your torso and hips in line

Keep your glutes and abs tight and your body in a relatively straight line during the entire movement. Don't allow your hips to sag and touch the ground, or raise up so high that they create an arch. If you have difficulty, try squeezing your glutes as you move.

 GENERAL TIP

Screw your hands into the ground to create more shoulder stability. This will help you prevent an injury and improve performance.

⚁ CHANGE IT UP

Hands-elevated push-up–If you struggle with normal push-ups, give hands-elevated push-ups a try. These are simply push-ups with your hands placed on a bench or the pin of a power rack to elevate your body. As the push-ups become easier, progressively lower the hands' elevation.

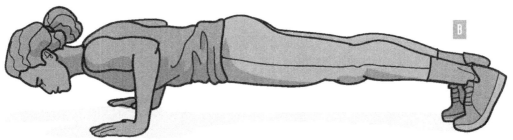

BARBELL BENCH PRESS

PRIMARY MUSCLES: CHEST

When training with the bench press, it is extremely important to dial in your form. Very few lifters outside of elite powerlifters understand all the variables of a proper bench press. Any breakdown in technique will quickly result in excessive soreness, poor performance, or even injury. Incorrect form causes shoulder injuries, but the bench can be a very safe lift if done correctly. It's responsible for more upper-body muscle growth than any other exercise, so it's worth doing well. SAFETY NOTE: Any time we are putting weight over our head, it's a good idea to have a spotter.

INSTRUCTIONS

1. Lie on a flat bench and position yourself so that your eyes are below the racked bar.

2. Before grasping the bar, arch your back, and squeeze together your shoulder blades. Think about trying to hold a pencil in your upper back. This is not only the most effective way to bench press the most weight; it also is the safest. Use your legs to help drive your upper back into the bench.

3. Once you are set, grasp the bar with an even grip that is slightly wider than your shoulders.

4. Lift the bar out of the rack, and position it over the chest with the arms fully extended. This is the starting position.

5. Take a deep breath, brace your core, and lower the bar to touch your chest at approximately the level of the nipples.

6. After a brief pause, push the bar back to the starting position. Focus on pushing the bar up and slightly back toward the rack.

7. Once you are back at the starting position, hold for one second, then start the next rep.

8. When you are done, place the bar back in the rack.

Common Mistakes and How to Avoid Them

Mistake 1: Butt coming off the bench

A common mistake on the bench press is allowing the butt to lift off the bench during the rep. This can lead not only to lower-back pain but also to a less effective bench press. The butt can rise for a few different reasons, but the most common is an incorrect leg drive.

Although the bench press is an upper-body lift, the lower body plays an important role. The more leg drive you use, the more weight you press. Remember, though, that you want to focus on pushing your toes through the front of your shoes. Tension should be going forward along the surface of the ground, not straight down. Getting this right can keep your butt on the bench and add pounds to the bar.

Mistake 2: Feet moving during the rep

The second most common mistake on the bench press is allowing your feet to move. Leg drive is important. If your feet are moving during the rep, this will severely limit how much weight you can lift. To prevent this, keep your feet flat on the floor at all times, and create tension in the lower body. You should be flexing your quads and glutes the entire time. If your lower body stays tight, it is almost impossible for your feet to move.

Mistake 3: Bouncing the bar off your chest

It's common for people to bounce the bar off their chests during each rep. Taking advantage of momentum is a way to lift more weight, but it creates a greater risk of injury, and it also limits how much chest activation you get from the exercise. Lower the weight in a slow and controlled manner. I recommend even pausing the bar for a second on your chest before returning to the starting position.

 GENERAL TIP

Where you grip the bar largely depends on personal preference and limb length. Generally speaking, longer arms require a wider grip. Play around with different grip widths until you find a position that is comfortable and allows you to lift the most weight.

CHANGE IT UP

Push-up—A great alternative to the bench press is the push-up, which is versatile and has many progressions and regressions (see here). A weight vest is the best way to add resistance; lack of resistance is the biggest limiting factor.

Smith machine bench press—If you struggle to balance the bar while bench pressing, it can help to use a Smith machine, which forces the bar into a vertical path.

DUMBBELL FLAT & INCLINE BENCH PRESS

PRIMARY MUSCLES: CHEST

These exercises are very similar to the barbell version, except that you use two dumbbells instead a barbell. The dumbbell variations allow for both sides of the chest to be worked equally, which can highlight any imbalance issues. Dumbbells also allow for a greater range of motion. The dumbbell incline bench press is my favorite incline variation to work the upper part of the chest. Adjust the bench angle to find what works best for you. I prefer an angle of less than 45 degrees.

INSTRUCTIONS

1. Sit on the edge of a flat or an incline bench with a dumbbell in each hand, resting on top of your knees. The palms of your hands should face each other.

2. Use your knees to help kick up the dumbbells. Lift them one at a time so that you can hold them at shoulder level.

3. Rotate your wrists forward so that the palms of your hands are facing away from you. This is the starting position.

4. To begin the movement, push the dumbbells up to full arm extension.

5. Once you reach full extension, slowly lower the weights back to the starting position.

Common Mistakes and How to Avoid Them

Mistake 1: Arching your back too much (incline dumbbell press)

On the incline dumbbell press, it's okay to retract your shoulders, but try to limit excessive arching. Arching takes tension off the upper chest and defeats the purpose of the exercise.

Mistake 2: Not using a full range of motion (flat dumbbell press)

One of the benefits of using dumbbells is that they allow for a greater range of motion. However, it's easy to cut the rep short because there is not a definitive endpoint (for example, a barbell touches your chest). Make sure you always use a full range of motion unless you are restricted by an injury.

 GENERAL TIP

Ask a gym partner or staff member to help you get the dumbbells into position. Also, if it feels more comfortable, you can press the dumbbells straight up with a neutral grip (palms facing each other) instead of using a pronated grip (see here).

🎲 CHANGE IT UP

Barbell incline bench press– The advantage of this barbell variation is that it allows you to use more weight. Be aware, however, that most barbell incline bench stations are set too high, which shifts more focus onto the shoulders instead of the chest.

Ring push-up–This is one of the best push-up variations as long as you properly adjust the height of the rings to your strength. The lower the rings, the more difficult the exercise. Once you have the rings set, grab one in each hand. Keeping your body straight and your legs fully extended behind you, perform a push-up.

Single-arm dumbbell bench press–The single-arm dumbbell bench press is a unique exercise I have been using with clients for years! It is performed the same way as a traditional dumbbell bench press, but you use only one dumbbell at a time. Before jumping into this one, choose a dumbbell that is considerably lighter than what you would regularly use with a dumbbell bench press.

CLOSE-GRIP BENCH PRESS

PRIMARY MUSCLES: CHEST AND TRICEPS

The close-grip bench press is a bench variation that works the triceps as much as the chest, if not more, and it's one of the best exercises to gain muscle in the triceps.

INSTRUCTIONS

1. Lie back on a flat bench and position your body so that your eyes are under the racked bar.

2. Before grasping the bar, arch your back, and squeeze together your shoulder blades. Think about trying to hold a pencil in your upper back. This is not only the most effective way to bench press the most weight; it also is the safest. Use your legs to help drive your upper back into the bench.

3. Once you are set, grasp the bar with a close grip that is slightly narrower than shoulder width.

4. Lift the bar out of the rack and position it over your chest with your arms fully extended. This is the starting position.

5. Take a deep breath, brace your core, and lower the bar to touch the middle part of your chest. Unlike the regular bench press, it's important to keep your elbows tucked in during the entire rep.

6. After a brief pause, push the bar back to the starting position. Focus on pushing the bar up and slightly back toward the rack.

7. Once you are back at the starting position, hold for one second and then start the next rep.

8. When you are done, place the bar back in the rack.

Common Mistakes and How to Avoid Them

Mistake: Gripping the bar too close

A common mistake with this bench press is actually gripping the bar with your hands too close together. Don't take the name "close grip" too literally. If your hands are too close together, it puts unneeded pressure on the wrists and limits how much weight you can use. You want to grip the bar only *slightly* narrower than shoulder width to gain the exercise benefits.

 GENERAL TIP

Try to set up and execute the lift the same way you would a regular bench press. The only tangible difference is the width of your grip.

CHANGE IT UP

Close-grip push-up—An excellent bodyweight variation, this movement is performed the same way as a traditional push-up, except that you place your hands closer together than shoulder width.

DUMBBELL PULLOVER

PRIMARY MUSCLES: CHEST AND LATS

The dumbbell pullover is another exercise that Arnold Schwarzenegger made famous in *Pumping Iron*, but I don't see it done much anymore, which is a shame. It's a unique chest exercise because it also works the lats and serratus. The dumbbell pullover also is one of the few chest exercises that doesn't involve any pressing, so it's easy on the elbows.

INSTRUCTIONS

1. Stand up a dumbbell vertically on a flat bench.

2. Lie perpendicular to the bench and keep only your shoulders and upper back on the surface. (Your head should be off the bench.) Your hips should be below the bench and your legs bent. Plant your feet firmly on the floor.

3. Hold the dumbbell with your palms pressing the underside. Slightly bending your arms, raise it above your chest. This is your starting position.

4. While keeping your bent arms locked in the starting position, slowly lower the weight in an arc behind your head until you feel a good stretch across your chest.

5. At that point, bring the dumbbell back in the same curving motion to the starting position.

Common Mistakes and How to Avoid Them

Mistake: Bending your arms too much

If the arms are bent too much during this exercise, it can become more of a triceps exercise, which is not what you want. The key is to maintain the same arm angle throughout the exercise.

 GENERAL TIP

Try to get as good a stretch at the bottom of the exercise as you can; don't shortchange the range of motion. As you pull the dumbbell up, flex the chest hard.

🔀 CHANGE IT UP

Pullover machine–Some gyms have a pullover machine, but keep in mind that it tends to target the lats in this exercise a little more than the chest. Adjust the seat so that your arms are flat on the pads and you are able to grasp the bar above with both hands while sitting. Pull the bar down, driving your arms and elbows into the pads. Pull down as far as the machine allows, then slowly bring the weight back to the starting position.

EZ curl bar pullover–Try doing pullovers with an EZ curl bar, which allows you to use a wider grip and may be more comfortable for your shoulders.

PARALLEL BAR DIP

PRIMARY MUSCLES: CHEST AND TRICEPS

The parallel bar dip is one the simplest but most effective chest exercises. Most gyms have a set of parallel bars for doing dips. Otherwise, you can make do by setting up two bars in a squat rack or using the backs of two chairs. The dip is also a terrific triceps builder.

INSTRUCTIONS

1. Stand between a set of parallel bars. Place a hand on each bar, and take a small jump to help you get into the starting position with your arms locked.

2. Begin by flexing the elbows and lowering your body until your arms break a 90-degree angle. To keep the stress on your chest, lean forward about 30 degrees and slightly flare your elbows out to the sides.

3. Reverse the motion by extending your elbows and pushing yourself back up into the starting position.

Common Mistakes and How to Avoid Them

Mistake: Staying too vertical

Maintaining a vertical torso during the movement makes it more of a triceps exercise. That's not necessarily bad technique, but you want to focus on the chest with dips. Make sure you lean forward at the waist and maintain that position throughout the entire movement. In addition, keep your lower body still. Avoid any leg kicking or swinging, to keep all the tension on the chest.

GENERAL TIP

To put extra emphasis on the chest, use the widest grip with which you can comfortably perform the exercise. The narrower the grip, the more your triceps will be engaged.

CHANGE IT UP

Weighted dip–If moving your bodyweight is too easy, you can use a weight belt to add more resistance, but don't be in a rush to add extra weight before you are ready. For most people, bodyweight dips provide plenty of resistance.

Assisted dip–On the other hand, if using your bodyweight is too difficult at first, you can do a machine-assisted dip. Push-ups are another great alternative.

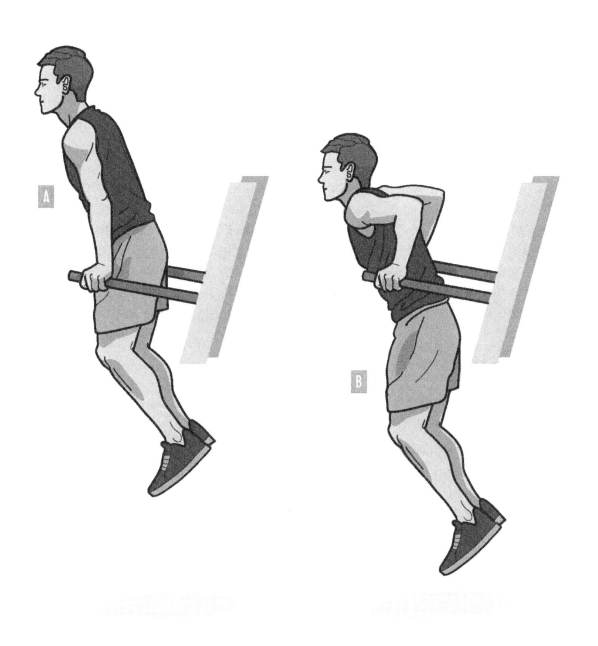

CABLE CROSSOVER FLY

PRIMARY MUSCLES: CHEST

I recommend very few isolation exercises for the chest, but the cable crossover fly is one of the best! The biggest advantage to using it versus dumbbells is that the cable provides constant tension. When the dumbbells are at the top in a fly, the weight primarily rests on the bones and joints, taking tension off of the muscle. In contrast, a cable crossover provides an equal amount of tension through the entire range of motion, which leads to more muscle activation.

INSTRUCTIONS

1. Start by placing two pulleys in a high position on opposite sides of the cable station.

2. Grab a pulley in each hand. Center yourself between the pulleys while drawing your arms together in front of you. Your torso should bend slightly forward from your waist. Keep your feet in a split stance with one foot in front of the other. This is your starting position.

3. With only a slight bend in your elbows, extend your arms to the sides in a wide arc until you feel a stretch across your chest.

4. Once your arms stretch back as far as they can, return to the starting position using the same arcing motion used to lower the weights.

5. Hold for one second at the starting position, then repeat.

Common Mistakes and How to Avoid Them

Mistake: Using a pressing motion versus a fly

The cable crossover is an exercise of finesse. Sure, you could move more weight by pressing, but that would defeat the purpose of the exercise. To get the most out of the movement, use an arcing motion, similar to hugging a big tree, and be sure to squeeze your chest hard at the top of the motion.

 GENERAL TIP

You can change the pulling angle of the cable from high to low (and anything in between) to change the effect of the exercise. Experiment with different angles, and find the one you like best.

CHANGE IT UP

Dumbbell fly–Although I prefer the cable version, a dumbbell fly is a good option if you don't have access to a cable machine. Lie on a flat bench with a dumbbell in each hand, palms facing each other and arms extended above your chest. Lower your arms to both sides in a wide arc until you feel a stretch across your chest. Use your chest to return the dumbbells in the same wide arc to the starting position.

Pec deck–This machine provides movement that is very similar to a cable crossover. Sit on the machine with your back flat against the pad and your hands grasping the handles. Push the handles toward the midline of your body. Once your hands come together, return slowly to the starting position.

MACHINE CHEST PRESS

PRIMARY MUSCLES: CHEST

The machine chest press is an easy-to-learn exercise that does a great job of adding more chest volume without needing to stabilize the weight as you would with barbells or dumbbells.

INSTRUCTIONS

1. Sit on the chest press machine, and select the weight.

2. Grab the handles with an overhand grip, and raise your elbows so that your upper arms are parallel to the floor. This is the starting position.

3. Push the handles away from you until you reach your full extension. Hold the end range for one second before returning to the starting position.

Common Mistakes and How to Avoid Them

Mistake: Not setting the seat pad correctly

One of the key elements to the machine chest press is getting the seat and back pad setting right for your size. If you incorrectly set the adjustments, you may not get the most out of the exercise. Make sure you can perform a full range of motion.

 GENERAL TIP

Since the machine chest press doesn't require any stabilization, it is one of the safer exercises in this book. It's an exercise you can push closer to muscle failure, especially on the last set.

🔀 CHANGE IT UP

Hammer Strength decline press–There are many different types of machine chest presses. If your gym has more than one, try them and use the one that is most comfortable. One of my favorites is the Hammer Strength decline press machine because it allows you to train in the decline pressing angle without all the blood rushing to your head.

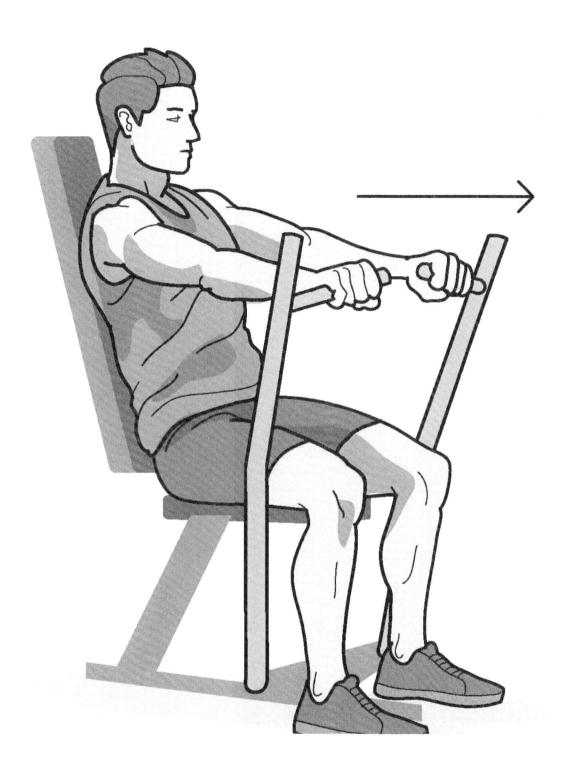

DOORWAY CHEST STRETCH

PRIMARY MUSCLES: CHEST

The doorway chest stretch is a simple stretch that can be done anywhere. I like to do this at the end of an upper-body workout to help open up the chest and shoulders area. Maintaining a good range of motion is critical to avoiding injury.

INSTRUCTIONS

1. Stand next to a doorway in a staggered stance. Extend your left arm out parallel to the floor, and place it on the door frame.

2. Turn your body away from your arm. Concentrate the stretch on the left pectoral and hold the position.

3. Repeat on the left side.

Common Mistakes and How to Avoid Them

Mistake: Keeping your arm totally locked out

Maintaining a slight elbow bend can allow for a better stretch.

 GENERAL TIP

Move your hand higher or lower on the doorway to change the focus of the stretch until you find the area that is tight.

 CHANGE IT UP

Behind-the-head chest stretch–Place your hands behind your head with your fingers interlocked. Pull your elbows back behind your ears and hold the stretched position.

PART THREE
THE 12-WEEK
JUMP-START PROGRAM

THE ULTIMATE GOAL of any bodybuilding program is to build as much muscle as possible. As a beginner, you have several areas to target. First, you want to develop a program that builds a base of strength and muscle across your entire body. It's pretty common for beginners to favor certain muscle groups they enjoy training, such as the arms or chest for men or the glutes for women. Balance is key, however. You don't want a training program that puts more emphasis on one body part than another.

Second, it's important to learn proper technique. The pointers in the previous section will certainly help, but practice is the key to mastery. Not only will correct form help prevent injuries, but it will also keep the tension on the targeted muscle group and away from the joints.

Third, and perhaps most important, you want to develop a habit of going to the gym and building consistency that lasts a lifetime. You can have the best program in the world on paper, but if it's not followed, that's not going to matter.

With this book, you'll accomplish your training goals with a 12-week training program consisting of three distinct phases. In Phase 1, you'll lay the foundation for your training and focus on developing the fundamentals. In Phase 2, you'll shift your focus to building muscle. And in Phase 3, you'll use that newly built muscle to work toward improved strength.

If you follow this program for the entire 12 weeks, you'll see noticeable changes in your body composition. Beyond that, I'm confident the habits and discipline you develop will help you continue your fitness journey for the rest of your life.

TRAINING PROGRAM NOTES:

- Take as much rest in between sets as you need on exercises that are not included in the circuits.
- Exercises within the circuits are meant to be done back-to-back with minimal rest.
- When you finish a circuit, take as much rest as you need before starting the next round.

PHASE 1: LAYING THE FOUNDATION

WEEK 1

The first week of any new program is the hardest. It's tough to develop new habits. Give yourself some slack; everything does not need to be perfect right off the bat. It's also important to remember that building muscle takes time, and there are no shortcuts when it comes to your body.

I know you are probably eager to see progress, and I don't blame you. Still, don't rush to add tons of weight to the bar. As a beginner, your body can respond quickly and make good progress using light weights. You don't need to break any records! Technique is of the utmost importance. Get comfortable with the exercises before adding weight. Week 1 is an introductory week, and you'll have plenty of time to work out more aggressively as you progress in the program.

DAY 1:
LEGS, GLUTES, AND ABS

THE WARM-UP

1. 5 minutes of light cardiovascular activity
2. Leg Swing: 2 sets of 10 (forward/back and side/side)
3. Air Squat: 2 sets of 10 reps

THE WORKOUT

1. Back Squat: 3 sets of 5 reps
2. Romanian Deadlift: 2 sets of 5 reps
3. Barbell Hip Thrust: 2 sets of 5 reps

Circuit (2 rounds of 8 to 10 reps)

4a. Seated Leg Curl
4b. Back Extension
4c. Forearm Plank: 30 to 60 seconds

1. Couch Stretch: 2 sets per side, with a 15 to 20 second hold each side
2. Hurdle Stretch: 2 sets per side, with a 15 to 20 second hold each side

 CHECK-IN

Starting today, you'll do a check-in every three weeks to monitor progress.

1. Check your bodyweight first thing in the morning, nude, after going to the bathroom.
2. Note: Due to normal daily fluctuations, a good habit to get into is checking your bodyweight under these conditions multiple times per week and calculating a weekly average. However, you'll analyze the weigh-ins only every few weeks.
3. Take photos of your body from the front, side, and rear. It's hard to see changes in your own physique since you see yourself every day, but your progress will be more apparent week-to-week.
4. Finally, take a few circumference measurements.

   Chest: Measure at the maximum horizontal girth of the chest at the nipple line. Breathe normally, stand up straight, and pass the tape measure under your armpits.

   Right Arm (flexed): Measure halfway between the elbow and the shoulder.

   Waist: Measure at the navel. Stand up straight and breath normally.

   Hips/Glutes: Measure around the glutes at the level of maximum circumference.

   Right Thigh: Measure at the halfway point between the center of the kneecap and the hip.

DAY 2:
UPPER BODY

THE WARM-UP

1. 5 minutes of light cardiovascular activity
2. Rope Lat Extension: 2 sets of 10 reps

3. Band Dislocation: 2 sets of 10 reps
4. Push-up: 2 sets of 5 to 10 reps (take 5 seconds to lower your body)

THE WORKOUT

1. Barbell Bench Press: 3 sets of 5 reps
2. Barbell Row: 3 sets of 5 reps

Circuit 1 (2 rounds of 8 reps)
  3a. Lat Pulldown
  3b. Dumbbell Side Raise
  3c. Cable Triceps Pressdown

Circuit 2 (2 rounds of 10 reps)
  4a. Dumbbell Flat & Incline Bench Press
  4b. EZ Bar Curl
  4c. Rope Face Pull

THE COOLDOWN

1. Doorway Chest Stretch: 2 sets per side of a 15 to 20 second hold
2. Lat Stretch: 2 sets per side of a 15 to 20 second hold
3. Dead Hang: 2 sets per side of a 10 to 30 second hold

DAY 3:
REST/RECOVERY

DAY 4:
LEGS, GLUTES, AND ABS

THE WARM-UP

1. 5 minutes of light cardiovascular activity
2. Leg Swing: 2 sets of 10 (forward/back and side/side)
3. Air Squat: 2 sets of 10 reps

THE WORKOUT

1. Deadlift: 3 sets of 5 reps
2. Dumbbell Bulgarian Split Squat: 2 sets of 8 reps

3. Leg Press: 2 sets of 8 reps
Circuit (2 rounds of 8 to 10 reps)
    4a. Leg Extension
    4b. Seated Calf Raise
    4c. Rope Cable Crunch

THE COOLDOWN

1. Couch Stretch: 2 sets per side, with a 15 to 20 second hold each side
2. Hurdle Stretch: 2 sets per side, with a 15 to 20 second hold each side

DAY 5:
FREE PLAY

Do something outside the gym today. This is a great day for "active recovery."
- Go for a long walk.
- Practice a martial art.
- Play a round of golf.
- Take a yoga class.

If you are in a fat-loss phase, you can use this as a cardio-only day.

DAY 6:
UPPER BODY

THE WARM-UP

1. 5 minutes of light cardiovascular activity
2. Rope Lat Extension: 2 sets of 10
3. Band Dislocation: 2 sets of 10 reps
4. Push-up: 2 sets of 5 to 10 reps (take 5 seconds to lower your body)

THE WORKOUT

1. Overhead Barbell Press: 3 sets of 5 reps
2. Dumbbell Row: 3 sets of 5 reps
Circuit 1 (2 rounds of 8 reps)

3a. Neutral-Grip Lat Pulldown
3b. Dumbbell Flat & Incline Bench Press
3c. Lying EZ Bar Triceps Extension

Circuit 2 (2 rounds of 10 reps)

4a. Dumbbell Shrug
4b. Dumbbell Hammer Curl
4c. Cable Side Raise

THE COOLDOWN

1. Doorway Chest Stretch: 2 sets per side of a 15 to 20 second hold
2. Lat Stretch: 2 sets per side of a 15 to 20 second hold
3. Dead Hang: 2 sets per side of a 15 to 20 second hold

DAY 7:
REST/RECOVERY

 FIT TIP:

Keep a training journal

Keep track of all of your workouts. You can use an app or go old school and use a composition notebook. Be as detailed as possible. Write down how much weight you used on each exercise, if the weights felt heavy or light, how much energy you had during the workout, etc. This information will be important in the coming weeks.

WEEK 2

Congratulations, you made it through the first week! The hardest part is over. Now you can start to build on what you did in Week 1.

During Week 2, you'll notice some exercises have additional sets, and the circuits have more rounds. This is one method of building progressive overload into the program. One of the fundamental principles of training is that you must do more work over time to make progress.

It's normal to have muscle aches the first week. The soreness will start to get better this week as your body adapts to the exercises.

DAY 8:
LEGS, GLUTES, AND ABS

THE WARM-UP

1. 5 minutes of light cardiovascular activity
2. Leg Swing: 2 sets of 10 (forward/back and side/side)
3. Air Squat: 2 sets of 10 reps

THE WORKOUT

1. Back Squat: 3 sets of 5 reps
2. Romanian Deadlift: 3 sets of 5 reps
3. Barbell Hip Thrust: 3 sets of 5 reps
Circuit (3 rounds of 8 to 10 reps)
   4a. Seated Leg Curl
   4b. Back Extension
   4c. Forearm Plank: 30 to 60 seconds
   4d. Bicycle Crunch

THE COOLDOWN

1. Couch Stretch: 2 sets per side, with a 15 to 20 second hold each side

2. Hurdle Stretch: 2 sets per side, with a 15 to 20 second hold each side

DAY 9:
UPPER BODY

THE WARM-UP
1. 5 minutes of light cardiovascular activity
2. Rope Lat Extension: 2 sets of 10 reps
3. Band Dislocation: 2 sets of 10 reps
4. Push-up: 2 sets of 5 to 10 reps (take 5 seconds to lower your body)

THE WORKOUT
1. Barbell Bench Press: 3 sets of 5 reps
2. Barbell Row: 3 sets of 5 reps

Circuit 1 (3 rounds of 8 reps)
- 3a. Lat Pulldown
- 3b. Dumbbell Side Raise
- 3c. Cable Triceps Pressdown

Circuit 2 (2 rounds of 10 reps)
- 4a. Dumbbell Bench Flat & Incline Press
- 4b. EZ Bar Curl
- 4c. Rope Face Pull

THE COOLDOWN
1. Doorway Chest Stretch: 2 sets per side of a 15 to 20 second hold
2. Lat Stretch: 2 sets per side of a 15 to 20 second hold
3. Dead Hang: 2 sets per side of a 15 to 20 second hold

DAY 10:
REST/RECOVERY

DAY 11:
LEGS, GLUTES, AND ABS

1. 5 minutes of light cardiovascular activity
2. Leg Swing: 2 sets of 10 (forward/back and side/side)
3. Air Squat: 2 sets of 10 reps

THE WORKOUT

1. Deadlift: 3 sets of 5 reps
2. Dumbbell Bulgarian Split Squat: 3 sets of 8 reps
3. Leg Press: 3 sets of 8 reps
Circuit (3 rounds of 8 to 10 reps)
    4a. Leg Extension
    4b. Seated Calf Raise
    4c. Rope Cable Crunch
    4d. Back-Supported Knee Raise

THE COOLDOWN

1. Couch Stretch: 2 sets per side, with a 15 to 20 second hold each side
2. Hurdle Stretch: 2 sets per side, with a 15 to 20 second hold each side

DAY 12:
FREE PLAY

Do something outside the gym today.

DAY 13:
UPPER BODY

THE WARM-UP

1. 5 minutes of light cardiovascular activity
2. Rope Lat Extension: 2 sets of 10 reps
3. Band Dislocation: 2 sets of 10 reps
4. Push-up: 2 sets of 5 to 10 reps (take 5 seconds to lower your body)

THE WORKOUT

1. Overhead Barbell Press: 3 sets of 5 reps
2. Dumbbell Row: 3 sets of 5 reps

Circuit 1 (3 rounds of 8 reps)
- 3a. Neutral-Grip Lat Pulldown
- 3b. Dumbbell Flat & Incline Bench Press
- 3c. Lying EZ Bar Triceps Extension

Circuit 2 (2 rounds of 10 reps)
- 4a. Dumbbell Shrug
- 4b. Dumbbell Hammer Curl
- 4c. Cable Side Raise

THE COOLDOWN

1. Doorway Chest Stretch: 2 sets per side of a 15 to 20 second hold
2. Lat Stretch: 2 sets per side of a 15 to 20 second hold
3. Dead Hang: 2 sets per side of a 15 to 20 second hold

DAY 14:
REST/RECOVERY

WEEK 3

As you begin Week 3, you should be feeling comfortable with the exercises. You've probably even noticed some physique changes. If not, don't worry. Remember, progress takes time. Trust the process and continue to be consistent.

Now that you have two weeks under your belt, I want you to focus on training density. Training density is the work you're able to do in a given amount of time. Keep track of when you start and finish each workout. Don't rush, but aim to be as efficient as possible. Attack the low-hanging fruit and limit how much time you take to socialize between sets or walk to the water fountain. Eliminating wasted time not only gets you in and out of the gym faster; it can also increase progress.

DAY 15:
LEGS, GLUTES, AND ABS

THE WARM-UP

1. 5 minutes of light cardiovascular activity
2. Leg Swing: 2 sets of 10 (forward/back and side/side)
3. Air Squat: 2 sets of 10 reps

THE WORKOUT

1. Back Squat: 4 sets of 5 reps
2. Romanian Deadlift: 3 sets of 5 reps
3. Barbell Hip Thrust: 3 sets of 5 reps
Circuit (3 rounds of 8 to 10 reps)
   - 4a. Seated Leg Curl
   - 4b. Back Extension
   - 4c. Forearm Plank: 30 to 60 seconds
   - 4d. Bicycle Crunch

THE COOLDOWN
1. Couch Stretch: 2 sets per side, with a 15 to 20 second hold each side
2. Hurdle Stretch: 2 sets per side, with a 15 to 20 second hold each side

DAY 16:
UPPER BODY

THE WARM-UP

1. 5 minutes of light cardiovascular activity
2. Rope Lat Extension: 2 sets of 10 reps
3. Band Dislocation: 2 sets of 10 reps
4. Push-up: 2 sets of 5 to 10 reps (take 5 seconds to lower your body)

THE WORKOUT

1. Barbell Bench Press: 3 sets of 5 reps
2. Barbell Row: 3 sets of 5 reps

Circuit 1 (3 rounds of 8 reps)
  3a. Lat Pulldown
  3b. Dumbbell Side Raise
  3c. Cable Triceps Pressdown

Circuit 2 (3 rounds of 10 reps)
  4a. Dumbbell Flat & Incline Bench Press
  4b. EZ Bar Curl
  4c. Rope Face Pull

THE COOLDOWN

1. Doorway Chest Stretch: 2 sets per side of a 15 to 20 second hold
2. Lat Stretch: 2 sets per side of a 15 to 20 second hold
3. Dead Hang: 2 sets per side of a 15 to 20 second hold

DAY 17:
REST/RECOVERY

 FIT TIP:

Focus on yourself

I know this may sound obvious, but I want you to focus on improving yourself throughout this entire process. It's easy to get sidetracked by what others do in the gym or what you see on social media. Everyone responds to training differently. Have confidence in yourself and aim to get a little better each week.

DAY 18:
LEGS, GLUTES, AND ABS

THE WARM-UP

1. 5 minutes of light cardiovascular activity
2. Leg Swing: 2 sets of 10 (forward/back and side/side)
3. Air Squat: 2 sets of 10 reps

THE WORKOUT

1. Deadlift: 4 sets of 5 reps
2. Dumbbell Bulgarian Split Squat: 3 sets of 8 reps
3. Leg Press: 3 sets of 8 reps
Circuit (3 rounds of 8 to 10 reps)
   4a. Leg Extension
   4b. Seated Calf Raise
   4c. Rope Cable Crunch
   4d. Back-Supported Knee Raise

THE COOLDOWN

1. Couch Stretch: 2 sets per side, with a 15 to 20 second hold each side
2. Hurdle Stretch: 2 sets per side, with a 15 to 20 second hold each side

DAY 19:
FREE PLAY

Do something outside the gym today.

DAY 20:
UPPER BODY

THE WARM-UP

1. 5 minutes of light cardiovascular activity
2. Rope Lat Extension: 2 sets of 10 reps
3. Band Dislocation: 2 sets of 10 reps
4. Push-up: 2 sets of 5 to 10 reps (take 5 seconds to lower your body)

THE WORKOUT

1. Overhead Barbell Press: 3 sets of 5 reps
2. Dumbbell Row: 3 sets of 5 reps

Circuit 1 (3 rounds of 8 reps)
    3a. Neutral-Grip Lat Pulldown
    3b. Dumbbell Flat & Incline Bench Press
    3c. Lying EZ Bar Triceps Extension

Circuit 2 (3 rounds of 10 reps)
    4a. Dumbbell Shrug
    4b. Dumbbell Hammer Curl
    4c. Cable Side Raise

THE COOLDOWN

1. Doorway Chest Stretch: 2 sets per side of a 15 to 20 second hold
2. Lat Stretch: 2 sets per side of a 15 to 20 second hold
3. Dead Hang: 2 sets per side of a 15 to 20 second hold

DAY 21:
REST/RECOVERY

 CHECK-IN

Let's see where you are after the first three weeks!

1. Check your bodyweight first thing in the morning, nude, after going to the bathroom.

2. Take photos of your body from the front, side, and rear.
3. Take a few circumference measurements.

   Chest: Measure at the maximum horizontal girth of the chest at the nipple line. Breathe normally, stand up straight, and pass the tape measure under the armpits.

   Right Arm (flexed): Measure halfway between the elbow and the shoulder.

   Waist: Measure at the navel. Stand up straight and breath normally.

   Hips/Glutes: Measure around the glutes at the level of maximum circumference.

   Right Thigh: Measure at the halfway point between the center of the kneecap and the hip.

WEEK 4

The first month of the program is almost over. Let's finish up this first phase strong! After 21 days, your daily habits are taking shape. Going to the gym and being consistent with your diet are becoming second nature. Don't let up. Discipline, like your biceps, needs to be trained.

One thing I want to point out before we jump into Week 4 is that you don't always need to suffer more in order to make progress. There are times when the workouts are going to be hard and feel uncomfortable, but for the most part the process should be enjoyable.

DAY 22:
LEGS, GLUTES, AND ABS

THE WARM-UP

1. 5 minutes of light cardiovascular activity
2. Leg Swing: 2 sets of 10 (forward/back and side/side)
3. Air Squat: 2 sets of 10 reps

THE WORKOUT

1. Back Squat: 4 sets of 5 reps
2. Romanian Deadlift: 3 sets of 5 reps
3. Barbell Hip Thrust: 3 sets of 5 reps
Circuit (4 rounds of 8 to 10 reps)
    4a. Seated Leg Curl
    4b. Back Extension
    4c. Forearm Plank: 30 to 60 seconds
    4d. Bicycle Crunch

THE COOLDOWN

1. Couch Stretch: 2 sets per side, with a 15 to 20 second hold each side

2. Hurdle Stretch: 2 sets per side, with a 15 to 20 second hold each side

DAY 23:
UPPER BODY

THE WARM-UP

1. 5 minutes of light cardiovascular activity
2. Rope Lat Extension: 2 sets of 10 reps
3. Band Dislocation: 2 sets of 10 reps
4. Push-up: 2 sets of 5 to 10 reps (take 5 seconds to lower your body)

THE WORKOUT

1. Barbell Bench Press: 4 sets of 5 reps
2. Barbell Row: 3 sets of 5 reps

Circuit 1 (4 rounds of 8 reps)
- 3a. Lat Pulldown
- 3b. Dumbbell Side Raise
- 3c. Cable Triceps Pressdown

Circuit 2 (3 rounds of 10 reps)
- 4a. Dumbbell Flat & Incline Bench Press
- 4b. EZ Bar Curl
- 4c. Rope Face Pull

THE COOLDOWN

1. Doorway Chest Stretch: 2 sets per side of a 15 to 20 second hold
2. Lat Stretch: 2 sets per side of a 15 to 20 second hold
3. Dead Hang: 2 sets per side of a 15 to 20 second hold

DAY 24:
REST/RECOVERY

DAY 25:
LEGS, GLUTES, AND ABS

1. 5 minutes of light cardiovascular activity
2. Leg Swing: 2 sets of 10 (forward/back and side/side)
3. Air Squat: 2 sets of 10 reps

THE WORKOUT

1. Deadlift: 4 sets of 5 reps
2. Dumbbell Bulgarian Split Squat: 3 sets of 8 reps
3. Leg Press: 3 sets of 8 reps
Circuit (4 rounds of 8 to 10 reps)
    4a. Leg Extension
    4b. Seated Calf Raise
    4c. Rope Cable Crunch
    4d. Back-Supported Knee Raise

THE COOLDOWN

1. Couch Stretch: 2 sets per side, with a 15 to 20 second hold each side
2. Hurdle Stretch: 2 sets per side, with a 15 to 20 second hold each side

DAY 26:
FREE PLAY

Do something outside the gym today.

DAY 27:
UPPER BODY

THE WARM-UP

1. 5 minutes of light cardiovascular activity
2. Rope Lat Extension: 2 sets of 10 reps
3. Band Dislocation: 2 sets of 10 reps
4. Push-up: 2 sets of 5 to 10 reps (take 5 seconds to lower your body)

THE WORKOUT

1. Overhead Barbell Press: 4 sets of 5 reps
2. Dumbbell Row: 3 sets of 5 reps

Circuit 1 (4 rounds of 8 reps)
   3a. Neutral-Grip Lat Pulldown
   3b. Dumbbell Flat & Incline Bench Press
   3c. Lying EZ Bar Triceps Extension

Circuit 2 (3 rounds of 10 reps)
   4a. Dumbbell Shrug
   4b. Dumbbell Hammer Curl
   4c. Cable Side Raise

THE COOLDOWN

1. Doorway Chest Stretch: 2 sets per side of a 15 to 20 second hold
2. Lat Stretch: 2 sets per side of a 15 to 20 second hold
3. Dead Hang: 2 sets per side of a 15 to 20 second hold

DAY 28:
REST/RECOVERY

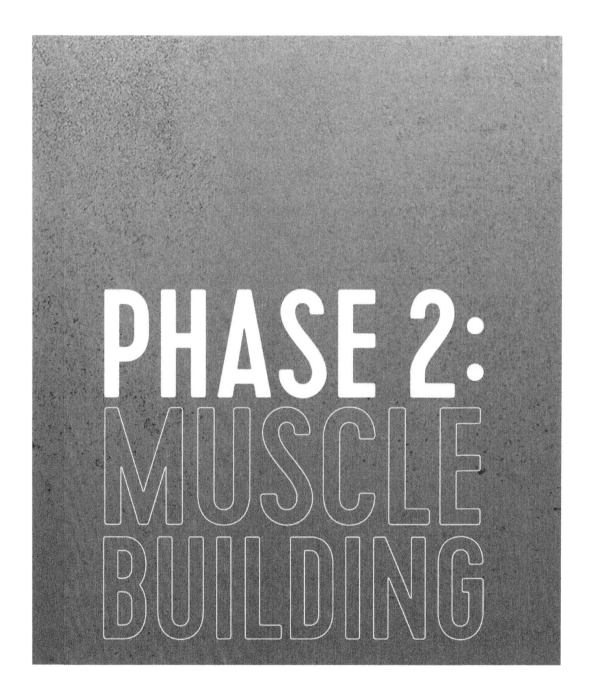

PHASE 2: MUSCLE BUILDING

WEEK 5

The base phase is over, and now you are ready to take the next step and focus on building muscle. By focusing on different adaptations, we're able to prevent lulls in progress.

In this phase, you'll notice higher reps because building muscle is largely about accumulating volume. (Volume is calculated by multiplying the number of sets by the reps by the weight.) The easiest way to increase volume is to increase the number of reps, but don't let that scare you.

Keep in mind that you need to use lighter weights when performing more reps, and the goal is always to lift heavier weights over time, regardless of the number of reps.

DAY 29:
LEGS, GLUTES, AND ABS

THE WARM-UP

1. 5 minutes of light cardiovascular activity
2. Leg Swing: 2 sets of 10 (forward/back and side/side)
3. Air Squat: 2 sets of 10 reps

THE WORKOUT

1. Back Squat: 3 sets of 8 reps
2. Dumbbell Step-up: up to 3 sets of 8 reps
3. Barbell Hip Thrust: 3 sets of 8 reps
Circuit (4 rounds of 10 to 12 reps)
   4a. Seated Leg Curl
   4b. Back Extension
   4c. Ab Wheel
   4d. Cable Pallof Press

THE COOLDOWN

1. Couch Stretch: 2 sets per side, with a 15 to 20 second hold each side
2. Hurdle Stretch: 2 sets per side, with a 15 to 20 second hold each side

DAY 30:
UPPER BODY

THE WARM-UP

1. 5 minutes of light cardiovascular activity
2. Rope Lat Extension: 2 sets of 10 reps
3. Band Dislocation: 2 sets of 10 reps
4. Push-up: 2 sets of 5 to 10 reps (take 5 seconds to lower your body)

THE WORKOUT

1. Close-Grip Bench Press: 3 sets of 8 reps
2. Dumbbell Incline Prone Row: 3 sets of 8 reps

Circuit 1 (4 rounds of 10 reps)
   3a. Pull-up
   3b. Dumbbell Side Raise
   3c. Cable Triceps Pressdown

Circuit 2 (3 rounds of 12 reps)
   4a. Machine Chest Press
   4b. EZ Bar Curl
   4c. Rope Face Pull

THE COOLDOWN

1. Doorway Chest Stretch: 2 sets per side of a 15 to 20 second hold
2. Lat Stretch: 2 sets per side of a 15 to 20 second hold
3. Dead Hang: 2 sets per side of a 15 to 20 second hold

DAY 31:
REST/RECOVERY

 FIT TIP:

Take a video of yourself lifting

If you struggle with a particular exercise, record a video of yourself performing the movement. Sometimes that can help you see where you are making a mistake.

DAY 32:
LEGS, GLUTES, AND ABS

THE WARM-UP

1. 5 minutes of light cardiovascular activity
2. Leg Swing: 2 sets of 10 (forward/back and side/side)
3. Air Squat: 2 sets of 10 reps

THE WORKOUT

1. Romanian Deadlift: 3 sets of 8 reps
2. Dumbbell Bulgarian Split Squat: 3 sets of 10 reps
3. Leg Press: 3 sets of 10 reps
Circuit (4 rounds of 10 to 12 reps)
   4a. Leg Extension
   4b. Seated Calf Raise
   4c. Decline Sit-up
   4d. Lying Leg Lift

THE COOLDOWN

1. Couch Stretch: 2 sets per side, with a 15 to 20 second hold each side
2. Hurdle Stretch: 2 sets per side, with a 15 to 20 second hold each side

DAY 33:
FREE PLAY

Do something outside the gym today.

DAY 34:
UPPER BODY

THE WARM-UP

1. 5 minutes of light cardiovascular activity
2. Rope Lat Extension: 2 sets of 10 reps
3. Band Dislocation: 2 sets of 10 reps
4. Push-up: 2 sets of 5 to 10 reps (take 5 seconds to lower your body)

THE WORKOUT

1. Seated Dumbbell Shoulder Press: 3 sets of 8 reps
2. Seated Cable Row: 3 sets of 8 reps

Circuit 1 (4 rounds of 10 reps)

3a. Single-Arm Lat Pulldown
3b. Cable Crossover Fly
3c. Parallel Bar Dip

Circuit 2 (3 rounds of 12 reps)

4a. Dumbbell Shrug
4b. Dumbbell Hammer Curl
4c. Cable Side Raise

THE COOLDOWN

1. Doorway Chest Stretch: 2 sets per side of a 15 to 20 second hold
2. Lat Stretch: 2 sets per side of a 15 to 20 second hold
3. Dead Hang: 2 sets per side of a 15 to 20 second hold

DAY 35:
REST/RECOVERY

WEEK 6

As you start Week 6, you'll notice the reps increase for certain exercises. They increase again in Week 8 to build more volume into the program as you continue to make progress.

During Phase 2, the concept of autoregulation is very important. It refers to your ability to adjust the workout program around how you feel day to day. Your readiness to work out depends on multiple factors, including nutrition, sleep, stress, and mood, and these will affect your performance. On days you feel good, get after it and push yourself a little harder. It's okay to adjust the workout on days you are not at your best. Be honest with yourself.

DAY 36:
LEGS, GLUTES, AND ABS

THE WARM-UP

1. 5 minutes of light cardiovascular activity
2. Leg Swing: 2 sets of 10 (forward/back and side/side)
3. Air Squat: 2 sets of 10 reps

THE WORKOUT

1. Back Squat: 3 sets of 10 reps
2. Dumbbell Step-up: 3 sets of 10 reps
3. Barbell Hip Thrust: 3 sets of 10 reps
Circuit (4 rounds of 10 to 12 reps)
   4a. Seated Leg Curl
   4b. Back Extension
   4c. Ab Wheel
   4d. Cable Pallof Press

THE COOLDOWN

1. Couch Stretch: 2 sets per side, with a 15 to 20 second hold each side

2. Hurdle Stretch: 2 sets per side, with a 15 to 20 second hold each side

DAY 37:
UPPER BODY

1. 5 minutes of light cardiovascular activity
2. Rope Lat Extension: 2 sets of 10 reps
3. Band Dislocation: 2 sets of 10 reps
4. Push-up: 2 sets of 5 to 10 reps (take 5 seconds to lower your body)

1. Close-Grip Bench Press: 3 sets of 10 reps
2. Dumbbell Incline Prone Row: 3 sets of 10 reps

Circuit 1 (4 rounds of 10 reps)
   3a. Pull-up
   3b. Dumbbell Side Raise
   3c. Cable Triceps Pressdown

Circuit 2 (3 rounds of 12 reps)
   4a. Machine Chest Press
   4b. EZ Bar Curl
   4c. Rope Face Pull

1. Doorway Chest Stretch: 2 sets per side of a 15 to 20 second hold
2. Lat Stretch: 2 sets per side of a 15 to 20 second hold
3. Dead Hang: 2 sets per side of a 15 to 20 second hold

DAY 38:
REST/RECOVERY

DAY 39:
LEGS, GLUTES, AND ABS

1. 5 minutes of light cardiovascular activity
2. Leg Swing: 2 sets of 10 (forward/back and side/side)
3. Air Squat: 2 sets of 10 reps

THE WORKOUT

1. Romanian Deadlift: 3 sets of 10 reps
2. Dumbbell Bulgarian Split Squat: 3 sets of 10 reps
3. Leg Press: 3 sets of 10 reps

Circuit (4 rounds of 10 to 12 reps)
   4a. Leg Extension
   4b. Seated Calf Raise
   4c. Decline Sit-up
   4d. Lying Leg Lift

THE COOLDOWN

1. Couch Stretch: 2 sets per side, with a 15 to 20 second hold each side
2. Hurdle Stretch: 2 sets per side, with a 15 to 20 second hold each side

DAY 40:
FREE PLAY

Do something outside the gym today.

DAY 41:
UPPER BODY

THE WARM-UP

1. 5 minutes of light cardiovascular activity
2. Rope Lat Extension: 2 sets of 10 reps
3. Band Dislocation: 2 sets of 10 reps
4. Push-up: 2 sets of 5 to 10 reps (take 5 seconds to lower your body)

THE WORKOUT

1. Seated Dumbbell Shoulder Press: 3 sets of 10 reps
2. Seated Cable Row: 3 sets of 10 reps

   Circuit 1 (4 rounds of 10 reps)

   3a. Single-Arm Lat Pulldown
   3b. Cable Crossover Fly
   3c. Parallel Bar Dip

   Circuit 2 (3 rounds of 12 reps)

   4a. Dumbbell Shrug
   4b. Dumbbell Hammer Curl
   4c. Cable Side Raise

THE COOLDOWN

1. Doorway Chest Stretch: 2 sets per side of a 15 to 20 second hold
2. Lat Stretch 2 sets per side of a 15 to 20 second hold
3. Dead Hang: 2 sets per side of a 15 to 20 second hold

DAY 42:
REST/RECOVERY

 CHECK-IN

1. Check your bodyweight first thing in the morning, nude, after going to the bathroom.
2. Take photos of your body from the front, side, and rear.
3. Next, take a few circumference measurements.

   Chest: Measure at the maximum horizontal girth of the chest at the nipple line. Breathe normally, stand up straight, and pass the tape measure under your armpits.

   Right Arm (flexed): Measure halfway between the elbow and the shoulder.

   Waist: Measure at the navel. Stand up straight and breathe normally.

   Hips/Glutes: Measure around the glutes at the level of maximum circumference.

   Right Thigh: Measure at the halfway point between the center of the kneecap and the hip.

WEEK 7

At the start of Week 7, you are officially halfway through the program. This is a perfect time to reflect on the previous six weeks. Take a look at your starting pictures and measurements from Day 1 and compare them to Day 42.

Analyze your progress so far: Are you on track to meet your goals by the end of Week 12? If so, great. Keep up the good work—there's no need to fix what's not broken. However, if you are not satisfied with your current progress, the good news is that you still have six more weeks. Use this time to refocus and recommit to the process. If you need to recalibrate, review your diet and nutrition. Depending on your goals, you may need to reduce calories to lose weight or increase calories to gain more muscle.

DAY 43:
LEGS, GLUTES, AND ABS

THE WARM-UP

1. 5 minutes of light cardiovascular activity
2. Leg Swing: 2 sets of 10 (forward/back and side/side)
3. Air Squat: 2 sets of 10 reps

THE WORKOUT

1. Back Squat: 4 sets of 10 reps
2. Dumbbell Step-up: 3 sets of 10 reps
3. Barbell Hip Thrust: 4 sets of 10 reps
Circuit (4 rounds of 10 to 12 reps)
    4a. Seated Leg Curl
    4b. Back Extension
    4c. Ab Wheel
    4d. Cable Pallof Press

1. Couch Stretch: 2 sets per side, with a 15 to 20 second hold each side
2. Hurdle Stretch: 2 sets per side with a 15 to 20 second hold each side

DAY 44:
UPPER BODY

THE WARM-UP

1. 5 minutes of light cardiovascular activity
2. Rope Lat Extension: 2 sets of 10 reps
3. Band Dislocation: 2 sets of 10 reps
4. Push-up: 2 sets of 5 to 10 reps (take 5 seconds to lower your body)

THE WORKOUT

1. Close-Grip Bench Press: 4 sets of 10 reps
2. Dumbbell Incline Prone Row: 4 sets of 10 reps

Circuit 1 (4 rounds of 10 reps)
- 3a. Pull-up
- 3b. Dumbbell Side Raise
- 3c. Cable Triceps Pressdown

Circuit 2 (3 rounds of 12 reps)
- 4a. Machine Chest Press
- 4b. EZ Bar Curl
- 4c. Rope Face Pull

THE COOLDOWN

1. Doorway Chest Stretch: 2 sets per side of a 15 to 20 second hold
2. Lat Stretch: 2 sets per side of a 15 to 20 second hold
3. Dead Hang: 2 sets per side of a 15 to 20 second hold

DAY 45:
REST/RECOVERY

 FIT TIP:

Track your daily steps

How you live your life outside the gym plays a large role in your fitness success, and a great way to measure your overall activity is tracking your daily steps. Most smartphones have a built-in app to track steps while the phone is on you and able to pinpoint your location. Aim to take between 8,000 and 10,000 steps per day.

DAY 46:
LEGS, GLUTES, AND ABS

THE WARM-UP

1. 5 minutes of light cardiovascular activity
2. Leg Swing: 2 sets of 10 (forward/back and side/side)
3. Air Squat: 2 sets of 10 reps

THE WORKOUT

1. Romanian Deadlift: 4 sets of 10 reps
2. Dumbbell Bulgarian Split Squat: 3 sets of 10 reps
3. Leg Press: 4 sets of 10 reps
Circuit (4 rounds of 10 to 12 reps)
   4a. Leg Extension
   4b. Seated Calf Raise
   4c. Decline Sit-up
   4d. Lying Leg Lift

THE COOLDOWN

1. Couch Stretch: 2 sets per side, with a 15 to 20 second hold each side
2. Hurdle Stretch: 2 sets per side, with a 15 to 20 second hold each side

DAY 47:
FREE PLAY

Do something outside the gym today.

DAY 48:
UPPER BODY

THE WARM-UP

1. 5 minutes of light cardiovascular activity
2. Rope Lat Extension: 2 sets of 10 reps
3. Band Dislocation: 2 sets of 10 reps
4. Push-up: 2 sets of 5 to 10 reps (take 5 seconds to lower your body)

THE WORKOUT

1. Seated Dumbbell Shoulder Press: 4 sets of 10 reps
2. Seated Cable Row: 4 sets of 10 reps
Circuit 1 (4 rounds of 10 reps)
   3a. Single-Arm Lat Pulldown
   3b. Cable Crossover Fly
   3c. Parallel Bar Dip
Circuit 2 (3 rounds of 12 reps)
   4a. Dumbbell Shrug
   4b. Dumbbell Hammer Curl
   4c. Cable Side Raise

THE COOLDOWN

1. Doorway Chest Stretch: 2 sets per side of a 15 to 20 second hold
2. Lat Stretch: 2 sets per side of a 15 to 20 second hold
3. Dead Hang: 2 sets per side of a 15 to 20 second hold

DAY 49:
REST/RECOVERY

WEEK 8

You've made it to the final week of Phase 2. This is the highest-volume portion of the entire training program. A lot of progress can be made this week, so take the workouts and recovery seriously. Aim to sleep eight hours per night, try to limit outside stress as much as possible, and make sure you hit your daily protein goals. Remember, your success requires consistency and attention to detail.

DAY 50:
LEGS, GLUTES, AND ABS

THE WARM-UP

1. 5 minutes of light cardiovascular activity
2. Leg Swing: 2 sets of 10 (forward/back and side/side)
3. Air Squat: 2 sets of 10 reps

THE WORKOUT

1. Back Squat: 4 sets of 12 reps
2. Dumbbell Step-up: 3 sets of 12 reps
3. Barbell Hip Thrust: 4 sets of 12 reps
Circuit (4 rounds of 10 to 12 reps)
    4a. Seated Leg Curl
    4b. Back Extension
    4c. Ab Wheel
    4d. Cable Pallof Press

THE COOLDOWN

1. Couch Stretch: 2 sets per side, with a 15 to 20 second hold each side
2. Hurdle Stretch: 2 sets per side, with a 15 to 20 second hold each side

DAY 51:

THE WARM-UP

1. 5 minutes of light cardiovascular activity
2. Rope Lat Extension: 2 sets of 10 reps
3. Band Dislocation: 2 sets of 10 reps
4. Push-up: 2 sets of 5 to 10 reps (take 5 seconds to lower your body)

THE WORKOUT

1. Close-Grip Bench Press: 4 sets of 12 reps
2. Dumbbell Incline Prone Row: 4 sets of 12 reps

Circuit 1 (4 rounds of 10 reps)
- 3a. Pull-up
- 3b. Dumbbell Side Raise
- 3c. Cable Triceps Pressdown

Circuit 2 (3 rounds of 12 reps)
- 4a. Machine Chest Press
- 4b. EZ Bar Curl
- 4c. Rope Face Pull

THE COOLDOWN

1. Doorway Chest Stretch: 2 sets per side of a 15 to 20 second hold
2. Lat Stretch: 2 sets per side of a 15 to 20 second hold
3. Dead Hang: 2 sets per side of a 15 to 20 second hold

DAY 52:
REST/RECOVERY

DAY 53:
LEGS, GLUTES, AND ABS

THE WARM-UP

1. 5 minutes of light cardiovascular activity
2. Leg Swing: 2 sets of 10 (forward/back and side/side)

3. Air Squat: 2 sets of 10 reps

1. Romanian Deadlift: 4 sets of 12 reps
2. Dumbbell Bulgarian Split Squat: 3 sets of 12 reps
3. Leg Press: 4 sets of 12 reps
Circuit (4 rounds of 10 to 12 reps)
    4a. Leg Extension
    4b. Seated Calf Raise
    4c. Decline Sit-up
    4d. Lying Leg Lift

THE COOLDOWN

1. Couch Stretch: 2 sets per side, with a 15 to 20 second hold each side
2. Hurdle Stretch: 2 sets per side, with a 15 to 20 second hold each side

DAY 54:
FREE PLAY

Do something outside the gym today.

DAY 55:
UPPER BODY

THE WARM-UP

1. 5 minutes of light cardiovascular activity
2. Rope Lat Extension: 2 sets of 10 reps
3. Band Dislocation: 2 sets of 10 reps
4. Push-up: 2 sets of 5 to 10 reps (take 5 seconds to lower your body)

THE WORKOUT

1. Seated Dumbbell Shoulder Press: 4 sets of 12 reps
2. Seated Cable Row: 4 sets of 12 reps
Circuit 1 (4 rounds of 10 reps)
    3a. Single-Arm Lat Pulldown

3b. Cable Crossover Fly
3c. Parallel Bar Dip

Circuit 2 (3 rounds of 12 reps)

4a. Dumbbell Shrug
4b. Dumbbell Hammer Curl
4c. Cable Side Raise

THE COOLDOWN

1. Doorway Chest Stretch: 2 sets per side of a 15 to 20 second hold
2. Lat Stretch: 2 sets per side of a 15 to 20 second hold
3. Dead Hang: 2 sets per side of a 15 to 20 second hold

DAY 56:
REST/RECOVERY

PHASE 3: STRENGTH BUILDING

WEEK 9

Here you are at Phase 3, when it's all about *building* strength and then *testing* your strength. You'll notice the number of reps is slightly lower to allow for heavier weights in this phase.

Strength is underrated in the bodybuilding world, but it provides many benefits. First, getting stronger—increasing the amount of weight used in a given number of sets and reps—is a way to increase training volume. Second, focusing on strength gives you more direction in the gym. It can be hard to stay on track when the only goal is to build muscle. Muscles grow slowly but strength gains are made more quickly and more visibly.

DAY 57:
LEGS, GLUTES, AND ABS

THE WARM-UP

1. 5 minutes of light cardiovascular activity
2. Leg Swing: 2 sets of 10 (forward/back and side/side)
3. Air Squat: 2 sets of 10 reps

THE WORKOUT

1. Back Squat: 4 sets of 7 reps
2. Dumbbell Step-up: 3 sets of 7 reps
3. Barbell Hip Thrust: 3 sets of 7 reps
Circuit (4 rounds of 8 to 10 reps)
   4a. Seated Leg Curl
   4b. Back Extension
   4c. Ab Wheel
   4d. Side Plank: 45 to 60 seconds

THE COOLDOWN

1. Couch Stretch: 2 sets per side, with a 15 to 20 second hold each side

2. Hurdle Stretch: 2 sets per side, with a 15 to 20 second hold each side

DAY 58:
UPPER BODY

THE WARM-UP
1. 5 minutes of light cardiovascular activity
2. Rope Lat Extension: 2 sets of 10 reps
3. Band Dislocation: 2 sets of 10 reps
4. Push-up: 2 sets of 5 to 10 reps (take 5 seconds to lower your body)

THE WORKOUT
1. Barbell Bench Press: 4 sets of 7 reps
2. Barbell Row: 4 sets of 7 reps
Circuit 1 (4 rounds of 8 reps)
   3a. Neutral-Grip Lat Pulldown
   3b. Dumbbell Side Raise
   3c. Cable Triceps Pressdown
Circuit 2 (3 rounds of 10 reps)
   4a. Dumbbell Pullover
   4b. EZ Bar Preacher Curl
   4c. Rope Face Pull

THE COOLDOWN
1. Doorway Chest Stretch: 2 sets per side of a 15 to 20 second hold
2. Lat Stretch: 2 sets per side of a 15 to 20 second hold
3. Dead Hang: 2 sets per side of a 15 to 20 second hold

DAY 59:
REST/RECOVERY

 FIT TIP:

Eat more protein and vegetables

Whatever your diet strategy, make it a goal to have at least one serving of protein and one serving of vegetables with every meal.

DAY 60:
LEGS, GLUTES, AND ABS

THE WARM-UP

1. 5 minutes of light cardiovascular activity
2. Leg Swing: 2 sets of 10 (forward/back and side/side)
3. Air Squat: 2 sets of 10 reps

THE WORKOUT

1. Deadlift: 4 sets of 7 reps
2. Romanian Deadlift: 3 sets of 7 reps
3. Dumbbell Bulgarian Split Squat: 3 sets of 7 reps

Circuit (4 rounds of 8 to 10 reps)

4a. Leg Extension
4b. Seated Calf Raise
4c. Decline Sit-up
4d. Hollow-Body Hold: 10 to 30 seconds

THE COOLDOWN

1. Couch Stretch: 2 sets per side, with a 15 to 20 second hold each side
2. Hurdle Stretch: 2 sets per side, with a 15 to 20 second hold each side

DAY 61:
FREE PLAY

Do something outside the gym today.

DAY 62:
UPPER BODY

1. 5 minutes of light cardiovascular activity
2. Rope Lat Extension: 2 sets of 10 reps
3. Band Dislocation: 2 sets of 10 reps
4. Push-up: 2 sets of 5 to 10 reps (take 5 seconds to lower your body)

THE WORKOUT

1. Overhead Barbell Press: 4 sets of 7 reps
2. Chest-Supported Row: 4 sets of 7 reps
Circuit 1 (4 rounds of 8 reps)
   3a. Lat Pulldown
   3b. Single-Arm Dumbbell Bench Press
   3c. Parallel Bar Dip
Circuit 2 (3 rounds of 10 reps)
   4a. Dumbbell Shrug
   4b. Dumbbell Hammer Curl
   4c. Cable Side Raise

THE COOLDOWN

1. Doorway Chest Stretch: 2 sets per side of a 15 to 20 second hold
2. Lat Stretch: 2 sets per side of a 15 to 20 second hold
3. Dead Hang: 2 sets per side of a 15 to 20 second hold

DAY 63:
REST/RECOVERY

 CHECK-IN

1. Check your bodyweight first thing in the morning, nude, after going to the bathroom.
2. Take photos of your body from the front, side, and rear.
3. Finally, take a few circumference measurements.
Chest: Measure at the maximum horizontal girth of the chest at the nipple line. Breathe normally, stand up straight, and pass the tape measure under your armpits.

Right Arm (flexed): Measure halfway between the elbow and the shoulder.

Waist: Measure at the navel. Stand up straight and breath normally.

Hips/Glutes: Measure around the glutes at the level of maximum circumference.

Right Thigh: Measure at the halfway point between the center of the kneecap and the hip.

WEEK 10

Entering Week 10, you'll focus on using more weight in the main exercises: squats, bench presses, deadlifts, and overhead presses. This does *not* mean you should let your form deteriorate. Increase the weight only if your technique is good and you are capable of lifting a heavier load.

In this phase, it's also important to keep detailed notes on each workout. Record how much weight you use for each exercise, how the weight felt, and whether you could have used more weight for the given number of reps. Use this information as a basis for selecting weights in subsequent weeks.

DAY 64:
LEGS, GLUTES, AND ABS

THE WARM-UP

1. 5 minutes of light cardiovascular activity
2. Leg Swing: 2 sets of 10 (forward/back and side/side)
3. Air Squat: 2 sets of 10 reps

THE WORKOUT

1. Back Squat: 4 sets of 5 reps
2. Dumbbell Step-up: 3 sets of 5 reps
3. Barbell Hip Thrust: 3 sets of 5 reps
Circuit (4 rounds of 8 to 10 reps)
   4a. Leg Curl
   4b. Back Extension
   4c. Ab Wheel
   4d. Side Plank: 45 to 60 seconds

THE COOLDOWN

1. Couch Stretch: 2 sets per side, with a 15 to 20 second hold each side

2. Hurdle Stretch: 2 sets per side, with a 15 to 20 second hold each side

DAY 65:
UPPER BODY

THE WARM-UP

1. 5 minutes of light cardiovascular activity
2. Rope Lat Extension: 2 sets of 10 reps
3. Band Dislocation: 2 sets of 10 reps
4. Push-up: 2 sets of 5 to 10 reps (take 5 seconds to lower your body)

THE WORKOUT

1. Barbell Bench Press: 4 sets of 5 reps
2. Barbell Row: 4 sets of 5 reps
Circuit 1 (4 rounds of 8 reps)
   3a. Neutral-Grip Lat Pulldown
   3b. Dumbbell Side Raise
   3c. Cable Triceps Pressdown
Circuit 2 (3 rounds of 10 reps)
   4a. Dumbbell Pullover
   4b. EZ Bar Preacher Curl
   4c. Rope Face Pull

THE COOLDOWN

1. Doorway Chest Stretch: 2 sets per side of a 15 to 20 second hold
2. Lat Stretch: 2 sets per side of a 15 to 20 second hold
3. Dead Hang: 2 sets per side of a 15 to 20 second hold

DAY 66:
REST/RECOVERY

DAY 67:
LEGS, GLUTES, AND ABS

1. 5 minutes of light cardiovascular activity
2. Leg Swing: 2 sets of 10 (forward/back and side/side)
3. Air Squat: 2 sets of 10 reps

THE WORKOUT

1. Deadlift: 4 sets of 5 reps
2. Romanian Deadlift: 3 sets of 5 reps
3. Dumbbell Bulgarian Split Squat: 3 sets of 5 reps
Circuit (4 rounds of 8 to 10 reps)
   4a. Leg Extension
   4b. Seated Calf Raise
   4c. Decline Sit-up
   4d. Hollow-Body Hold: 10 to 30 seconds

THE COOLDOWN

1. Couch Stretch: 2 sets per side, with a 15 to 20 second hold each side
2. Hurdle Stretch: 2 sets per side, with a 15 to 20 second hold each side

DAY 68:
FREE PLAY

Do something outside the gym today.

DAY 69:
UPPER BODY

THE WARM-UP

1. 5 minutes of light cardiovascular activity
2. Rope Lat Extension: 2 sets of 10 reps
3. Band Dislocation: 2 sets of 10 reps
4. Push-up: 2 sets of 5 to 10 reps (take 5 seconds to lower your body)

THE WORKOUT

1. Overhead Barbell Press: 4 sets of 5 reps
2. Chest-Supported Row: 4 sets of 5 reps
Circuit 1 (4 rounds of 8 reps)
    3a. Lat Pulldown
    3b. Single-Arm Dumbbell Bench Press
    3c. Parallel Bar Dip
Circuit 2 (3 rounds of 10 reps)
    4a. Dumbbell Shrug
    4b. Dumbbell Hammer Curl
    4c. Cable Side Raise

THE COOLDOWN

1. Doorway Chest Stretch: 2 sets per side of a 15 to 20 second hold
2. Lat Stretch: 2 sets per side of a 15 to 20 second hold
3. Dead Hang: 2 sets per side of a 15 to 20 second hold

DAY 70:
REST/RECOVERY

WEEK 11

You're almost done! Over the last 10 weeks, you've laid the foundation for your training, built muscle, and gained strength. The last two weeks is where it all comes together.

Week 11 is one of the most important and challenging weeks in the entire program. The weights are going to be heavy. Focus on doing everything you can to maximize your performance in the gym. Continue to build on what you have accomplished and finish strong.

DAY 71:
LEGS, GLUTES, AND ABS

THE WARM-UP

1. 5 minutes of light cardiovascular activity
2. Leg Swing: 2 sets of 10 (forward/back and side/side)
3. Air Squat: 2 sets of 10 reps

THE WORKOUT

1. Back Squat: 4 sets of 3 reps
2. Dumbbell Step-up: 3 sets of 5 reps
3. Barbell Hip Thrust: 3 sets of 5 reps
Circuit (4 rounds of 8 to 10 reps)
   4a. Seated Leg Curl
   4b. Back Extension
   4c. Ab Wheel
   4d. Side Plank: 45 to 60 seconds

THE COOLDOWN

1. Couch Stretch: 2 sets per side, with a 15 to 20 second hold each side
2. Hurdle Stretch: 2 sets per side, with a 15 to 20 second hold each side

DAY 72:

THE WARM-UP

1. 5 minutes of light cardiovascular activity
2. Rope Lat Extension: 2 sets of 10 reps
3. Band Dislocation: 2 sets of 10 reps
4. Push-up: 2 sets of 5 to 10 reps (take 5 seconds to lower your body)

THE WORKOUT

1. Barbell Bench Press: 4 sets of 3 reps
2. Barbell Row: 4 sets of 5 reps
Circuit 1 (4 rounds of 8 reps)
    3a. Neutral-Grip Lat Pulldown
    3b. Dumbbell Side Raise
    3c. Cable Triceps Pressdown
Circuit 2 (3 rounds of 10 reps)
    4a. Dumbbell Pullover
    4b. EZ Bar Preacher Curl
    4c. Rope Face Pull

THE COOLDOWN

1. Doorway Chest Stretch: 2 sets per side of a 15 to 20 second hold
2. Lat Stretch: 2 sets per side of a 15 to 20 second hold
3. Dead Hang: 2 sets per side of a 15 to 20 second hold

DAY 73:

REST/RECOVERY

 FIT TIP:

Use a spotter

Make sure you have a spotter when you're doing heavy sets. If you're not working out with a training partner, don't be afraid to ask someone at the gym to assist you. Having a spotter not only keeps you safe; it also helps you perform better because you'll know you have assistance should you need it.

DAY 74:
LEGS, GLUTES, AND ABS

THE WARM-UP
1. 5 minutes of light cardiovascular activity
2. Leg Swing: 2 sets of 10 (forward/back and side/side)
3. Air Squat: 2 sets of 10 reps

THE WORKOUT
1. Deadlift: 4 sets of 3 reps
2. Romanian Deadlift: 3 sets of 5 reps
3. Dumbbell Bulgarian Split Squat: 3 sets of 5 reps
Circuit (4 rounds of 8 to 10 reps)
    4a. Leg Extension
    4b. Seated Calf Raise
    4c. Decline Sit-up
    4d. Hollow-Body Hold: 10 to 30 seconds

THE COOLDOWN
1. Couch Stretch: 2 sets per side, with a 15 to 20 second hold each side
2. Hurdle Stretch: 2 sets per side, with a 15 to 20 second hold each side

DAY 75:
FREE PLAY

Do something outside the gym today.

DAY 76:
UPPER BODY

THE WARM-UP

1. 5 minutes of light cardiovascular activity
2. Rope Lat Extension: 2 sets of 10 reps
3. Band Dislocation: 2 sets of 10 reps
4. Push-up: 2 sets of 5 to 10 reps (take 5 seconds to lower your body)

THE WORKOUT

1. Overhead Barbell Press: 4 sets of 3 reps
2. Chest-Supported Row: 4 sets of 5 reps

Circuit 1 (4 rounds of 8 reps)
- 3a. Lat Pulldown
- 3b. Single-Arm Dumbbell Bench Press
- 3c. Parallel Bar Dip

Circuit 2 (3 rounds of 10 reps)
- 4a. Dumbbell Shrug
- 4b. Dumbbell Hammer Curl
- 4c. Cable Side Raise

THE COOLDOWN

1. Doorway Chest Stretch: 2 sets per side of a 15 to 20 second hold
2. Lat Stretch: 2 sets per side of a 15 to 20 second hold
3. Dead Hang: 2 sets per side of a 15 to 20 second hold

DAY 77:
REST/RECOVERY

WEEK 12

You made it! Welcome to Week 12, a great opportunity to test your abilities and measure your progress.

In terms of testing, you have a few options. Each training day this week, you can use the main exercise of the day to work up to a 1-rep max (the heaviest weight you can do for one rep) or a 3- to 5-rep max (the heaviest weight you can lift for three to five reps). It's up to you. Most people are best served by the multiple-reps option, but if you feel comfortable doing a 1-rep max, go for it.

After you finish the program, take a couple of days off to rest and recover. When you're ready to return to the gym, go back to Day 1 and start again—only this time, aim to beat the lifting record you just set.

DAY 78:
LEGS, GLUTES, AND ABS

THE WARM-UP

1. 5 minutes of light cardiovascular activity
2. Leg Swing: 2 sets of 10 (forward/back and side/side)
3. Air Squat: 2 sets of 10 reps

THE WORKOUT

1. Back Squat: 1 set of 1 rep or 1 set of 3 to 5 reps
   (Work up to a 1-rep max or your heaviest set of 3 to 5 reps.)
2. Dumbbell Step-up: 2 sets of 5 reps
3. Barbell Hip Thrust: 2 sets of 5 reps
Circuit (2 rounds of 8 to 10 reps)
   4a. Leg Curl
   4b. Back Extension
   4c. Ab Wheel
   4d. Side Plank: 45 to 60 seconds

1. Couch Stretch: 2 sets per side, with a 15 to 20 second hold each side
2. Hurdle Stretch: 2 sets per side, with a 15 to 20 second hold each side

DAY 79:
UPPER BODY

THE WARM-UP

1. 5 minutes of light cardiovascular activity
2. Rope Lat Extension: 2 sets of 10 reps
3. Band Dislocation: 2 sets of 10 reps
4. Push-up: 2 sets of 5 to 10 reps (take 5 seconds to lower your body)

THE WORKOUT

1. Barbell Bench Press: 1 set of 1 rep or 1 set of 3 to 5 reps
   (Work up to a 1-rep max or your heaviest set of 3 to 5 reps.)
2. Barbell Row: 3 sets of 5 reps

Circuit 1 (3 rounds of 8 reps)
   3a. Neutral-Grip Lat Pulldown
   3b. Dumbbell Side Raise
   3c. Cable Triceps Pressdown

Circuit 2 (2 rounds of 10 reps)
   4a. Dumbbell Pullover
   4b. EZ Bar Preacher Curl
   4c. Rope Face Pull

THE COOLDOWN

1. Doorway Chest Stretch: 2 sets per side of a 15 to 20 second hold
2. Lat Stretch: 2 sets per side of a 15 to 20 second hold
3. Dead Hang: 2 sets per side of a 15 to 20 second hold

DAY 80:
REST/RECOVERY

DAY 81:

THE WARM-UP

1. 5 minutes of light cardiovascular activity
2. Leg Swing: 2 sets of 10 (forward/back and side/side)
3. Air Squat: 2 sets of 10 reps

THE WORKOUT

1. Deadlift: 1 set of 1 rep or 1 set of 3 to 5 reps
   (Work up to a 1-rep max or your heaviest set of 3 to 5 reps.)
2. Romanian Deadlift: 2 sets of 5 reps
3. Dumbbell Bulgarian Split Squat: 2 sets of 5 reps

Circuit (3 rounds of 8 to 10 reps)
   4a. Leg Extension
   4b. Seated Calf Raise
   4c. Decline Sit-up
   4d. Hollow-Body Hold: 10 to 30 seconds

THE COOLDOWN

1. Couch Stretch: 2 sets per side, with a 15 to 20 second hold each side
2. Hurdle Stretch: 2 sets per side, with a 15 to 20 second hold each side

DAY 82:
FREE PLAY

Do something outside the gym today.

DAY 83:
UPPER BODY

THE WARM-UP

1. 5 minutes of light cardiovascular activity

266

2. Rope Lat Extension: 2 sets of 10 reps
3. Band Dislocation: 2 sets of 10 reps
4. Push-up: 2 sets of 5 to 10 reps (take 5 seconds to lower your body)

THE WORKOUT

1. Overhead Barbell Press: 1 set of 1 rep or 1 set of 3 to 5 reps
   (Work up to a 1-rep max or your heaviest set of 3 to 5 reps.)
2. Chest-Supported Row: 3 sets of 5 reps

Circuit 1 (3 rounds of 8 reps)
   - 3a. Lat Pulldown
   - 3b. Single-Arm Dumbbell Bench Press
   - 3c. Parallel Bar Dip

Circuit 2 (2 rounds of 10 reps)
   - 4a. Dumbbell Shrug
   - 4b. Dumbbell Hammer Curl
   - 4c. Cable Side Raise

THE COOLDOWN

1. Doorway Chest Stretch: 2 sets per side of a 15 to 20 second hold
2. Lat Stretch: 2 sets per side of a 15 to 20 second hold
3. Dead Hang: 2 sets per side of a 15 to 20 second hold

DAY 84:
REST/RECOVERY

 CHECK-IN

By this point, you already know your strength gains. Now let's see your physique improvements!

1. Check your bodyweight first thing in the morning, nude, after going to the bathroom.
2. Take photos of your body from the front, side, and rear.
3. Finally, take a few circumference measurements.

   Chest: Measure at the maximum horizontal girth of the chest at the nipple line. Breathe normally, stand up straight, and pass the tape measure under your armpits.

Right Arm (flexed): Measure halfway between the elbow and the shoulder.

Waist: Measure at the navel. Stand up straight and breath normally.

Hips/Glutes: Measure around the glutes at the level of maximum circumference.

Right Thigh: Measure at the halfway point between the center of the kneecap and the hip.

Compare your bodyweight, photos, and circumference measurements to the first check-in on Day 1.

I want to congratulate you on finishing the 12-week program. You did it! You're in control now, and I hope you use what you have learned in this book to continue your bodybuilding journey.

Wishing you a life filled with fitness, health, and happiness,

CONCLUSION

Congratulations on reaching the culmination of "The Ultimate Bodybuilding Guide for Beginners." Your journey through the pages of this comprehensive guide has been more than a mere exploration of exercises and nutritional guidelines; it has been a transformative odyssey, laying the foundation for a healthier, stronger, and more resilient version of yourself.

Reflecting on the Journey

As you stand at the precipice of this conclusion, take a moment to reflect on the path you've traversed. You began with an understanding of bodybuilding beyond mere aesthetics, delving into the profound impact it can have on your mental, emotional, and physical well-being. The journey unfolded, guiding you through the intricacies of bodybuilding science, the importance of setting personal goals, and the art of tracking your progress. Each chapter was a stepping stone, building upon the last, as you set the stage for a holistic bodybuilding experience.

Mastering Techniques and Fundamental Exercises

The exploration of essential techniques and fundamental exercises has armed you with the knowledge needed to sculpt your body effectively. From dynamic leg swings to intricate cable crossover fly movements, you've learned to engage various muscle groups with precision and purpose. The chapters on leg development, back sculpting, shoulder and arm building, chest enhancement, core strengthening, and flexibility have provided a comprehensive toolkit for achieving a balanced and symmetrical physique.

The 12-Week Jump-Start Program: A Blueprint for Success

The heart of this guide lies in the 12-week jump-start program – a meticulously crafted blueprint designed to propel you toward tangible results. Week by week, you challenged your body, progressively increasing the intensity and pushing your limits. The incorporation of periodization ensured that your muscles were continually stimulated, preventing plateaus and promoting sustained growth.

As you navigated through the program, you discovered the importance of mental resilience and the mind-muscle connection. These psychological aspects of bodybuilding are often underestimated but are crucial for achieving optimal results. Your mental fortitude was put to the test, and you emerged not only physically stronger but mentally tougher, ready to face challenges beyond the gym.

Nourishing Your Body: Nutrition and Meal Prepping

A robust physique is not built on exercise alone but also on a foundation of proper nutrition. The chapters dedicated to nutrition provided essential guidelines for fueling your body, understanding macronutrients, and making informed choices. The art of meal prepping became a skill you mastered, transforming nutrition from a chore into a seamless and enjoyable part of your daily routine.

Adapting the Program to Your Unique Journey

Bodybuilding is a personal journey, and the flexibility of the 12-week program allowed you to adapt it to your unique needs. You learned to listen to your body, make adjustments based on progress, and overcome unforeseen challenges. This adaptability is a testament to the sustainability of the bodybuilding lifestyle – it's not a rigid set of rules but a dynamic and evolving process tailored to your individual growth.

The Importance of Recovery and Lifelong Learning

Balancing intensity with proper recovery emerged as a theme throughout this guide. You discovered the significance of sleep, active recovery days, and the necessity of allowing your body the time it needs to repair and grow. This understanding of recovery is a valuable lesson that extends beyond the confines of bodybuilding, impacting your overall well-being.

In recognizing that your bodybuilding journey is a lifelong learning process, you've embraced the idea that growth is continuous. As you celebrate your achievements, acknowledge that there is always room for improvement, new goals to pursue, and deeper insights to gain. The journey doesn't end here; it evolves, and you evolve with it.

Integrating Bodybuilding into Your Lifestyle

271

This guide isn't just about the 12-week program; it's about integrating bodybuilding into your lifestyle. The habits you've cultivated during this journey are not temporary measures but sustainable practices that contribute to your long-term health and fitness. Explore ways to seamlessly weave bodybuilding principles into your daily life, making fitness an integral part of who you are.

Inspiring Others and Building a Community

Now equipped with knowledge, experience, and a transformed physique, consider the impact you can have on others. Share your success story, inspire those around you, and contribute to building a community of like-minded individuals. The support and motivation derived from a community can elevate your journey and the journeys of those you inspire.

The Ever-Evolving Journey of Bodybuilding

In closing, this guide serves as a compass for the ever-evolving journey of bodybuilding. Embrace the constant evolution of your goals, techniques, and understanding of your body. Allow each milestone to propel you forward, knowing that the transformative power of bodybuilding extends beyond the physical – it reshapes your mindset, fortifies your spirit, and fosters a holistic sense of well-being.

As you turn the final page of this guide, remember that your bodybuilding journey is not a destination but a continuous expedition toward self-improvement. Embrace the challenges, celebrate the victories, and revel in the realization that you possess the knowledge and strength to sculpt the ultimate version of yourself. The echoes of your bodybuilding journey will resonate in your daily life, shaping not only your physique but also your character and resilience.

Thank you for entrusting "The Ultimate Bodybuilding Guide for Beginners" to be your companion on this transformative odyssey. May your future endeavors be filled with strength, vitality, and the enduring pursuit of personal excellence.

Embracing the Lifestyle Beyond the Gym

Your journey in bodybuilding has extended far beyond the gym walls. As you conclude this guide, consider how the principles you've embraced can influence your lifestyle. The discipline, dedication, and resilience cultivated in the pursuit of physical excellence can permeate other aspects of your life. The mindset of a bodybuilder transcends the weights – it becomes a guiding force in your professional pursuits, personal relationships, and overall approach to challenges.

Harnessing Mental Resilience for Life's Challenges

Bodybuilding isn't just about physical strength; it's a mental game as well. The mental resilience you've developed during this journey serves as a powerful tool for navigating life's challenges. As you encounter obstacles and setbacks outside the gym, draw upon the strength of mind cultivated in every squat, deadlift, and pull-up. Your newfound mental toughness is a resource that extends far beyond the realm of bodybuilding.

The Journey's Impact on Overall Well-Being

Reflect on the holistic impact of your bodybuilding journey on your overall well-being. Beyond the aesthetic improvements, consider how your energy levels, mood, and sleep patterns have evolved. The positive changes you've experienced in physical health are likely mirrored by improvements in mental and emotional well-being. The interconnected nature of wellness is a fundamental principle of bodybuilding that carries over into all aspects of your life.

Nurturing a Positive Body Image and Self-Esteem

One of the often-overlooked benefits of bodybuilding is its profound impact on body image and self-esteem. As you conclude this guide, take a moment to appreciate the newfound respect and love for your body. The sculpting process is not just external; it extends inward, fostering a positive relationship with yourself. Acknowledge and celebrate your body for its resilience, strength, and the journey it has undertaken.

Setting New Horizons: Lifelong Learning and Growth

The end of this guide marks not a conclusion but a commencement of new horizons. The bodybuilding journey is a lifelong expedition of learning and growth. As you move forward, embrace the thrill of setting new goals, exploring different training modalities, and pushing the boundaries of your capabilities. The bodybuilder's mindset is one of perpetual improvement – a philosophy that can shape a life of continuous learning and personal evolution.

Building Resilient Habits for a Lifetime

The habits cultivated during the 12-week program and the entirety of this guide are the building blocks of a resilient and healthy lifestyle. Whether it's the consistency of your workout routine, the precision of your nutrition choices, or the mindfulness of your recovery practices, these habits lay the foundation for a lifetime of well-being. Recognize the transformative power of habit and its capacity to shape your days, weeks, and years ahead.

Gratitude for the Transformative Journey

Express gratitude for the transformative journey you've experienced. From the initial pages that introduced you to the philosophy of bodybuilding to the final weeks of the 12-week jump-start program, every chapter has contributed to your growth. Be thankful for the challenges that tested your resolve, the successes that fueled your motivation, and the knowledge gained that empowers you to take charge of your health and fitness.

Continuity of Support and Inspiration

As you bid farewell to this guide, remember that the journey doesn't end here; it merely transforms. Stay connected to the community you've built, drawing inspiration from the stories and successes of others. Whether it's through online forums, local fitness groups, or personal connections, the continuity of support is a powerful motivator. Share your experiences, offer encouragement, and contribute to the ongoing narrative of transformation within the bodybuilding community.

The Legacy of Your Bodybuilding Odyssey

In concluding this guide, recognize that you are now part of a legacy – a legacy of individuals who have embraced the transformative power of bodybuilding. Your journey contributes to a tapestry of stories, each unique yet interconnected by the common pursuit of self-improvement. As you move forward, carry the torch of this legacy, inspiring others to embark on their own odyssey of growth, resilience, and personal excellence.

The Final Rep: A New Beginning

In the language of bodybuilding, the final repetition of a set is often the most challenging, pushing the muscles to their limits. As you conclude this guide, consider it your final rep – the culmination of efforts, the peak of accomplishment. But in the spirit of bodybuilding, this conclusion is not an endpoint; it's a platform for a new beginning. The weight of your achievements serves as resistance, propelling you forward into a future rich with possibilities, growth, and the unwavering pursuit of your best self.

Thank you for entrusting "The Ultimate Bodybuilding Guide for Beginners" to be your guide, companion, and source of inspiration.

May your journey continue to unfold with strength, resilience, and an unwavering commitment to the pursuit of greatness. The echoes of your bodybuilding odyssey reverberate not just in the gym but in the tapestry of your life – a testament to the transformative power within you.

Printed in Great Britain
by Amazon

56550976R00165